D1358669

the HOLISTIC GUIDE to DECLUTTERING

———————

Inspiring | Educating | Creating | Entertaining

Brimming with creative inspiration, how-to projects, and useful information to enrich your everyday life, Quarto Knows is a favorite destination for those pursuing their interests and passions. Visit our site and dig deeper with our books into your area of interest: Quarto Creates, Quarto Cooks, Quarto Homes, Quarto Lives, Quarto Drives, Quarto Explores, Quarto Gifts, or Quarto Kids.

© 2020 Quarto Publishing Group USA Inc.
Text © 2020 Michele Vig

First Published in 2020 by Fair Winds Press, an imprint of The Quarto Group, 100 Cummings Center, Suite 265-D, Beverly, MA 01915, USA. T (978) 282-9590 F (978) 283-2742 QuartoKnows.com

All rights reserved. No part of this book may be reproduced in any form without written permission of the copyright owners. All images in this book have been reproduced with the knowledge and prior consent of the artists concerned, and no responsibility is accepted by producer, publisher, or printer for any infringement of copyright or otherwise, arising from the contents of this publication. Every effort has been made to ensure that credits accurately comply with information supplied. We apologize for any inaccuracies that may have occurred and will resolve inaccurate or missing information in a subsequent reprinting of the book.

Fair Winds Press titles are also available at discount for retail, wholesale, promotional, and bulk purchase. For details, contact the Special Sales Manager by email at specialsales@quarto.com or by mail at The Quarto Group, Attn: Special Sales Manager, 100 Cummings Center, Suite 265-D, Beverly, MA 01915, USA.

24 23 22 21 20   1 2 3 4 5

ISBN: 978-1-59233-961-7

Digital edition published in 2020
eISBN: 978-1-63159-891-3

Library of Congress Cataloging-in-Publication Data

Vig, Michele, author.
Holistic guide to decluttering : organize and transform your space,
   time, and mind / Michele Vig.
ISBN 9781592339617 | ISBN 9781631598913 (eISBN)
1. House cleaning. 2. Orderliness. 3. Time management. 4. Storage
   in the home.
LCC TX324 .V54 2020 (print) | LCC TX324 (ebook) | DDC 648/.5--dc23

LCCN 2020003979 (print) | LCCN 2020003980 (ebook) |

Design and Page Layout: Tanya Jacobson, jcbsn.co
Photography: Jes Lahay, except pages 29, 40, 111, 133, 134, 171, 186, 188, 200 Shutterstock

Printed in China

the HOLISTIC GUIDE to DECLUTTERING

Organize and Transform Your Space, Time, and Mind

MICHELE VIG *of Neat little Nest*

FAIR WINDS

CONTENTS

INTRODUCTION

There are many organizing companies and plenty of resources that teach decluttering. In my own pursuit to learn as much as I could, I've read books on how to declutter, how to organize, how to simplify, how to prioritize . . . and the list goes on. While I'm grateful and appreciative for all I have learned, I found myself feeling there was something missing.

You see, I've always had a passion for organizing. I leveraged that passion to help keep my busy home life and calendar running smoothly during my twenty-year corporate career. I eventually followed my passion and took the leap to start my own organizing business. Now my life is all about helping others declutter and get organized.

As a professional organizer, I've witnessed the weight of physical clutter firsthand. I've seen it in my clients' eyes when we've met, and I've heard it in their voices. Physical clutter is heavy, anxiety triggering, and overwhelming. Fortunately, I've also seen how anxiety and stress can melt away when those same people spend focused time and energy decluttering and creating organizational systems.

I've found that decluttering physical things has had a positive impact for my clients, but too often it seemed its reach was not deep enough. A cluttered house might be resolved, but the change would not be lasting. In a house full of stress-inducing calendars and racing minds, the clean, organized home was only a temporary anchor. I realized that most people's focus was on the clutter we can see: the surface-level clutter.

Eventually, something clicked for me. The truth is that clutter is not always physical. Clutter is bigger than just "stuff." When you consider clutter holistically, you can see there are three main forms of clutter—physical, time, and mental—and they are all intricately linked.

It is my hope that this book will show you how all these types of clutter can be resolved. By decluttering holistically in all key areas, I hope to provide you with transformational change. We will start by examining the sources of clutter from a higher-level view, then get into the home. I'll help you sort through the most common areas where physical clutter builds up. I'll also share popular, proven strategies for organizing, as well as tactics to help you keep it that way. In the chapters that follow, we'll dig into the idea of the calendar and time budgeting to help free you from another key source of stress. Finally, we'll address what may be the most important topic of all: mental clutter.

My hope is that you will find inspiration in the pages that follow and that they will serve as a spark to help you dig deep into the different types of clutter that might be holding you back from living your most desired life. Ultimately, my goal is for you to expand your belief of what it means to live clutter free.

Let the holistic decluttering journey begin!

Michele Vig

CLUTTER GENESIS

It's important to consider what factors contributed to your clutter if you want to achieve lasting change.

Where does clutter begin? That's a difficult question to answer as every person's story is unique and multifaceted. With my clients, I have found one thing to be true: Everyone's life experiences and priorities are different. Furthermore, because we are exploring three areas of clutter in this book that are different, but intricately linked, guessing one root to the clutter is nearly impossible.

Let's look at physical clutter as an example. Some people have a lot of physical clutter simply because they buy a lot of stuff and have a difficult time managing it all. Others struggle with physical clutter because they have a difficult time letting things go—even when they know they need to. And the reasons don't stop there. There may be significant life events that disrupt routines and require a lot of time and focus, which lead to clutter. Or a racing mind and an inability to stay focused long enough to tend to the day-to-day needs could also be a factor.

In this chapter, we'll take a closer look at the reasons people find themselves buried in clutter. Some of the factors and stories may resonate with you, while others may not. My hope is that you will find both hope and inspiration in the chapters that follow. This chapter may help you understand how you got here—and you'll see you are certainly not alone.

- *When you only keep the items you love and can fit in the space, you'll ward off mountains of stress and clutter.*

Buying as a Source of Clutter

Before the Industrial Revolution, most people lived on or very close to the land that provided their food and didn't own or use many items that came from outside their community. Things have changed! New ways to manufacture and distribute products in the late 1800s and early 1900s had a significant impact on what people were able to buy, and then new technologies of the late 1900s and early 2000s had a large impact on how people were (and are) able to buy. Today, most of us can buy anything our hearts desire from across the globe at any hour of the day and have it shipped to our homes with the click of a few buttons.

However, just because we can buy more, and it's easier to do so, doesn't mean we should buy more. It's clear we have the freedom to choose and decide what we consume, so then why are we, as a society, deciding to take the path of overconsumption? No one is forcing us to buy more things than we can properly take care of or to spend money we don't have to buy things we don't actually need.

The reasons why we buy a lot of stuff are varied, personal, and often intertwined. As I reflected upon my buying habits, along with what I've learned from conversations with my family, friends, and clients about their buying habits, I've seen the following themes:

- We buy because we can.
- Salespeople and advertisements are powerful persuaders.
- We're trying to keep up with family, friends, neighbors, and colleagues.
- We're searching for happiness.

Buying to showcase your personal style can be a joyful experience as long as you can manage and take care of all of those items.

We Buy Because We Can

The number of dual-income families has been growing steadily since the 1970s, which, in turn, allows more families the financial means to buy more than the generation before them.

In fact, even if a person or family doesn't have the money in their bank accounts to buy what they want, the ability to buy is still there! Many people take out loans or use credit cards to buy the things on their wish list. In the United States, for example, the average consumer credit card debt at the time of this writing is close to $9,000, which equals more than $1 trillion in total credit card debt for the country. That number exceeds the record set in 2008, before the Great Recession. Before the 1950s, credit cards were almost nonexistent, which meant if you wanted to buy something you didn't have the money for, it was much harder to do so.

The Power of Persuasion

The sales and advertising industries are built on the power of persuasion. Getting someone to buy something is the purpose of both of these industries. Just walk into a car dealership, a clothing store, or any commission-based retailer, and you'll quickly see the power of persuasion firsthand. But the only one who really knows what is best for you is you.

When my husband and I were buying our second home, our realtor consistently showed us homes well above the price range we were comfortable spending—sometimes 25 to 50 percent higher. At first, we thought it was a simple misunderstanding. (The maximum budget my husband and I had set to purchase our house was well below the amount of money the bank said they would lend us.) Yet after many weeks of looking at overpriced homes and reminding our realtor of our budget, we started thinking maybe it was less of a misunderstanding and more that our realtor had hopes that we would overspend our budget. She would, of course, benefit financially if we did so. At this point, we had a very direct conversation with our realtor about our maximum price, which led to a souring of our relationship.

Thankfully, my husband and I stuck to our budget and found a home on our terms. However, I (and everyone else I know) have plenty of other examples of items I've purchased after being persuaded by a salesperson. Some of my regret-filled purchases include an expensive vacuum from an in-home salesperson, a leopard-print shirt that the saleswomen gushed over when I tried it on, and basically anything I've purchased from a home-based party where the host is a good friend—talk about the pressure to buy! And if the power of persuasion from salespeople weren't pressure enough, we also have the pressure from the marketing and advertising industries. The amount of money companies invest into advertising is astonishing, and they do it for one simple reason—it works.

Before I founded my business, Neat Little Nest, I worked in marketing and advertising for twenty years. Early in my career, I worked at an advertising agency where my job was to plan where to spend the media dollars in an effort to drive reach and frequency of the advertising message in order to increase traffic and sales for my client's product or retail store. We researched what types of ads were best, when to run those ads, and where to put the ads.

When I left the advertising agency, my career took me to the brands themselves. I worked inside the marketing departments of some amazing retail brands where we directed how and where to spend advertising dollars, along with designing stores for optimal sales. We researched and tested exactly where to place items in the store with a goal to increase impulse buying, which worked.

Sales and advertising cannot be faulted for why we're a cluttered-filled nation, but they do supply fuel to the consumerism fire. Advertising executives might claim they're trying to fulfill unmet needs of the consumer, but that's not always the reality. Quite a bit of advertising is created to get you to try something you've been living without just fine or to convince you an item you have is out of date and must be replaced.

If you don't think ads affect you, think again. Take a moment to consider the impact of advertising on you and your family. Think about the volume of advertising you see and hear everyday on TV, the radio, social media, and billboards. Now think about the events you attend, the clothes you wear, and the stores you drive by. All of those have advertising, too. I had a friend who had portions of her wedding paid for by sponsors as long as she advertised their products at the wedding!

Being a conscientious consumer is part of holistic decluttering, so it's important to become (or remain) conscious about advertising and how it can persuade you to buy things you may not need for reasons you might not have even considered before the advertising exposure.

Searching for Happiness

There are many parts of the world where shopping has become entertainment in and of itself. While shopping malls in the United States may have seen brighter days, shopping malls in other parts of the world, such as the United Arab Emirates, are booming. Not only can shopping be a social event and entertainment, it also can make us happier.

When we shop, the brain chemical dopamine is triggered. When we consider buying something new, the neurotransmitter surges as if the brain is anticipating a reward. If that new item is on the sale rack, the dopamine spikes more. Subconsciously, your brain calculates how buying an object of desire will feel even before you consciously consider whether to purchase it. For many, the shopping high is fleeting and leaves as quickly as it comes, leading to few personal challenges.

For some, the desire to continually feel the shopping high is tied to a deeper personal challenge that can lead to overconsumption and, in turn, clutter. People might buy things because they are trying to fill a void that has nothing at all to do with the item they are buying—and just like that, shopping can become an addiction.

Keeping Up With the Joneses

The phrase "Keeping up with the Joneses" originates from a comic strip with the same name created by Arthur R. "Pop" Momand in 1913. The strip ran in *New York World* and various other newspapers until the 1940s. In many parts of the English-speaking world, the phrase refers to comparing one's social status to that of one's neighbors based off of their possessions alone.

In the neighborhood where I grew up, one thing was clear—my family was *not* the Joneses. From what I could tell, we lived smack dab in between two "Jones" families. On one side of our house lived a family whose two daughters seemed to be treated like royalty. They dressed up to go to the movies, they had all of the latest toys, and both girls had their own walk-in closets next to makeup vanities with a sink!

On the other side of us was a prosperous family of five. Everything about their house was beautiful. It smelled nice, it looked nice, and everything was beautifully decorated. My jealousy in wanting to keep up with these neighbors often showed up during the back-to-school and Christmas seasons. And, as a result, I had a difficult time as a child managing the feelings of being "less than."

As an adult, I understand that I didn't have all the information needed to guide me to a place of loving wholeness.

- I didn't realize (or believe) that a person's value in this world is because of his or her unique gifts rather than being like the Joneses.
- I didn't realize that the Joneses' life might not be as idyllic as I had imagined.
- I didn't know if the Joneses could actually afford all of those things I couldn't have or if it was smoke and mirrors fueled by credit card debt.

No matter who the Joneses are in your life, trying to keep up with them is never a winning proposition. You will find that even if you try, there will always be someone else with something else that will stir up envy. It is a cycle that will never end.

The pull of keeping up with the Joneses is strong—for many, it is more powerful than advertising. Without clarity about what you desire in your own life, you can easily become adrift. This is why digging deep into what you desire is the first step in holistic decluttering. It will anchor you along the journey.

Keeping as a Source of Clutter

Buying a lot of stuff does not, on its own, always lead to clutter. Some people buy plenty but donate or sell their old items when they are done using them. They might have a revolving door of a closet, but it's not cluttered.

But that's not most people. The more common situation is that if you buy a lot, you probably keep a lot of it. Just as with buying, the reasons we keep a lot are varied, personal, and intertwined. In my life and with my business, I've seen attachment, as well as fear and guilt, play the largest roles.

Attachment

Our relationship with stuff starts early in our lives and it's a complicated one. As early as age two, children grasp the idea that they can own things. Just ask any preschool teacher if you doubt this to be true. Most children have an intense relationship with one or more attachment objects. Attachment objects are also called comfort or transitional objects, or security blankets. They are items used to provide psychological comfort, especially in unusual situations, or at bedtime.

In a 2007 study, Bruce Hood and Paul Bloom explored the bias in young children of preferring their own object to an identical duplicate item. What they learned, not surprisingly, is that children with attachment objects preferred their original object to a duplicate. None of the children offered a detailed rationale for their choice; they typically said the reason they liked it was because it was theirs.

• *Consider keeping a smaller number of memory items, but put them on display in a small vignette so you can see them often rather than having them tucked into a bin and never looked at again.*

CLIENT CHRONICAL: DROWNING IN GRAPHIC T-SHIRTS

One of my clients, we'll call him Dave, had a closet and a dresser that were overflowing. As we started to declutter, he said goodbye to a fair number of clothing items that no longer served the life he was living.

When we started sorting his graphic T-shirts, we had a considerable number to review. He had probaby 100 different T-shirts from concerts, coffee houses, family trips, etc. At first, he didn't want to let many of the T-shirts go.

I encouraged Dave to take a closer look at the T-shirts because the reality was that we couldn't fit everything he wanted to keep in the space. When he asked how many would fit into the space, I told him the number was about half of what he currently had. I gave him some alternatives to consider like making a quilt from the T-shirts or getting rid of more from other categories. I told him that without doing something different, he'd still have an overstuffed closet. Something had to give.

Armed with all of the information, he was able to take a fresh look at the stack of T-shirts and began to let even more of them go. He realized he was holding onto some of them more out of habit than an intentional love of the item. Once he'd put his space and options into consideration, it was easier for him to detach from the items and let enough go so that he could have the closet of his dreams.

Sometimes we are *afraid* we will hurt

our friends' and family's feelings if we don't

keep something they gave us,

but the act of giving the item was the gift.

If it no longer serves you,

your friends and family should be

the first ones to understand.

As children grow into teenagers, there are signs that their stuff is correlated to their identity and also to their self-esteem. This correlation continues in the transition from adolescence to adulthood and even as they begin "adulting." How much we see our things as an extension of our self-identity may depend in part on how confident we feel about who we are. The more confident we are in our self-identity, the easier it is to have some distance between ourselves and our things. The attachment we have to possessions is what makes it difficult for many to get rid of things even if we rationally know we have too much.

Fear (and Guilt)

There are many different reasons people are afraid to let things go, but in this section, I want to focus on three: fear of needing an object again and not having it, the scarcity mindset, and guilt. All of these fears get in the way of letting things go, which can lead to clutter-filled homes and garages.

One of the most common things I see as a professional organizer is the draw of the "I might need it someday" thinking. It's a slippery slope. On the one hand, you might need something you discard someday in the future. On the other hand, it is much more likely that someday will never come, especially for items you haven't used in years. Sometimes, this thinking is a result of a scarcity mindset.

A scarcity mindset is the belief that there will never be enough—whether it's money, food, or something else. The scarcity mindset is rooted in fear and often in past experience, but it's distinct from the fear of simply needing to use an item again in the future. I've worked with clients who exhibited a scarcity mindset even when it was quite clear that, financially speaking, they had nothing to be concerned about. A scarcity mindset can have quite a grip on your mental capacity to have hope.

You can always find reasons to keep things you no longer want rather than walk through the fear and other feelings and simply make the decision based on your own heart. The more you listen to your own heart and move in the direction of your dreams and not someone else's, the more free you will feel.

Guilt is a strong emotion and comes up during every single decluttering project without fail. Even when I think a project is simple and straightforward, guilt rears its ugly head. It is a major reason people hold onto things they don't actually like. I've seen many people keep items they don't like just because they think someone's feelings will be hurt if they chose to get rid them. More times than I can count, they will keep the items tucked in a box in the basement. I've had people tell me they'd rather hold onto an item until someone dies than confront the idea of getting rid of it while the person is still alive. Unfortunately, kicking guilt down the road doesn't make it go away. Facing it squarely and being honest allows you to detach from the guilt.

MOVING FORWARD

Cling to your dreams, not to your clutter.

The first time I heard the word "metanoia" was during a church service when the pastor was talking just with the children. During his message, the children were instructed to line up in a row behind the pastor and to follow him as he walked around the space. They were told to keep following him until he shouted the word "metanoia!" At that point, they were to turn around quickly and change directions. Each time he shouted "metanoia!" the children would quickly change directions, walking a new path.

The visual of the children quickly changing directions was a powerful demonstration of how easy change can be. It just takes one simple decision to change directions and go a different way—even though it doesn't always feel like it's that simple.

The deeper meaning of "metanoia" is to have a transformative change of heart. This subtle difference between simply changing directions to a transformative change of heart is what makes changing directions difficult in practice. To have a transformative change of heart, you must be more open and willing to face fears and anxieties that may hold you back. You must have faith and trust that where you are going is better than where you are today.

When your life is full of clutter—whether it be physical clutter, time clutter, or mental clutter—it becomes a barrier between you and the life you've always dreamed about. In order to move forward and get to a different place, you must make real changes. It requires you to fully embrace a new mindset. On the deepest level, it requires metanoia, a transformative change of heart.

In this chapter, you will learn more about how clutter affects you and those around you, how decluttering holistically can help you transform yourself and your life, and most importantly, you will begin to do work to envision your most desired life. Envisioning your most desired life will help reframe your view, which will allow you to move forward one decluttered step at a time.

- *Time and space will always give you a fresh perspective and the ability to move forward in a positive way.*

For many,
clutter is a source of

anxiety and stress

because the accumulation is

hidden behind closed doors.

The Grip of Physical Clutter

The grip of clutter can sometimes be difficult to understand, but it becomes clearer when you look at the science behind it. Clutter can trigger your body's fight-or-flight response by releasing cortisol—the stress hormone. This is especially true for women, according to a UCLA study by the Center of Everyday Lives of Families, where they found a link between how women describe their homes, a depressed mood, and cortisol levels.

Interestingly enough, the UCLA study also found that men who live in cluttered homes don't have the same increased levels of cortisol around clutter that women do. In other words, clutter affects men and women differently.

If you live in an environment that is in a perpetual state of clutter, your cortisol levels can stay perpetually elevated—and your body was not designed for that. Cortisol levels are supposed to spike in the morning to get you going and taper off as the day goes on.

This ongoing elevated cortisol puts you in a state of chronic stress, which can result in higher levels of depression and anxiety and inhibits your ability to think clearly, make decisions, and stay focused. What's worse, chronic stress can be the very thing that makes you feel so overwhelmed that you feel you don't have the emotional energy to change.

Just like any other stress, the stress from clutter can trigger unhealthy coping and avoidance strategies like eating junk food, oversleeping, and binge-watching TV, according to a study conducted by Cornell University in 2016.

The great news is that an earlier study showed that a person's mindset can serve as a buffer to unhealthy habits, which is why it's so important to consider all aspects of clutter—physical, time, and mental—when searching for a solution to declutter for good.

The Full Picture

It can be frustrating if you've decluttered in the past but haven't quite been able to make it stick. Many books on decluttering and organizing focus on the magical things that should happen when you declutter your space, and if that doesn't happen for you, you could feel like you've failed. Well, you haven't.

While some people might have transformational experiences simply from decluttering their physical environments, not everyone does. Clutter is not a one-size-fits-all issue. Clutter is multidimensional, which is why a holistic approach helps. When you dig into the different dimensions of clutter, it will be easier for you to unlock your full potential and live your most desired life.

Let's take a closer look at the three dimensions of clutter.

Three Dimensions of Clutter

There are three primary dimensions of clutter—physical, time, and mental.

Physical clutter is the clutter you can see in your home, car, and work-space. Time clutter is the clutter that happens on your calendar—being overscheduled and not planning ahead or reflecting back. Mental clutter is the clutter in your mind—the rushing thoughts, the mental to-do list, the never-ending noise in the mind.

● *Physical clutter is one of the three dimensions of clutter. It may seem like the easiest to tackle, but when you only focus on one area of clutter, you might not see the full effect clutter has in your life.*

Three Dimensions of Clutter

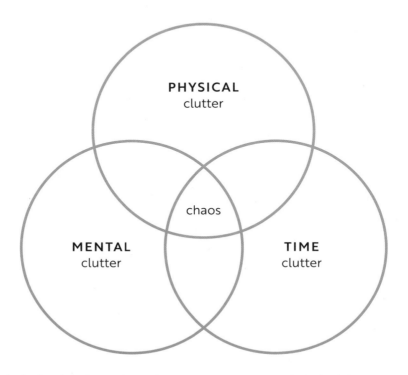

My belief is that these three dimensions are intricately linked. Having them all cluttered up at the same time feels chaotic.

Consider all of the decluttering you've done up to this point in your life. How much of it was focused on physical clutter compared to time clutter and mental clutter? I would guess you haven't really considered time clutter and mental clutter too much.

I'm here to suggest that time clutter and mental clutter might be at the root of your clutter challenge. Tackle physical clutter without considering the impact of the other two types of clutter on you and your life and you might find your decluttering regimes and organizing systems won't stick.

There are many positive things that can come from digging into the three dimensions of clutter, but the best thing that can happen is that through the process, you will learn more about yourself and begin to grow and change in ways you might never have imagined.

Dig deep inside yourself to find the roots of your clutter challenge because the answers always lie within.

Find the Root

I once worked with an amazing leader named Leigh Anne who consistently asked her team to dig to find the root cause of any problem because without finding the root cause, the team would simply waste its time and effort. The same applies to clutter.

Let's take a garden as a metaphorical example for clutter. If you see weeds (clutter) in your garden and run outside and cut off (declutter) the tops of the weeds, your garden will look weed free. However, it will only look good for a short amount of time since you left the roots in the soil. The weeds will come back and clutter up the garden again and again.

When you declutter holistically, you will dig deeper into your metaphorical garden. And, in doing so, you will begin to find which clutter dimension has the deepest root for you. Then you can take the necessary steps to see a full transformation in your life that will stick, allowing you the freedom to live your most desired life and to answer the call of your soul.

What to Expect (The Benefits)

Because I'm a professional organizer, people call me to help them get to a better place, and they share a lot of challenging clutter stories with me. While some who call are already filled with light energy and hope, many others feel like they are carrying a heavy burden.

But here's the thing. I only feel hope. I feel hope because I know that just around the corner their lives will be filled with a little more peace, happiness, and joy simply because our team will help them declutter and organize their space. It happens every time.

Gain Clearer Focus

It can be difficult to concentrate in a cluttered environment because clutter competes for your attention and can restrict your ability to focus. In a Princeton study, researchers mapped the brain's response to organized and disorganized stimuli while monitoring performance on tasks. The results showed that decluttered workspaces allow people to focus and process information better. This, in turn, can make people less irritable and more productive.

Clearing clutter is transformative and allows you to enjoy your space in a new way.

When you're in a cluttered space, it's as if the clutter is saying "Look at me! Look at me! Look at me!" This creates visual noise. This visual noise makes it difficult for you to concentrate because there is too much stimuli. Visual noise can wear down your mental resources until you feel exhausted.

Removing items from an overly cluttered room creates space. It creates space in your home, but it also opens up space in your mind. As you make decisions about what to keep and what to let go of, you begin to cross things off your mental to-do list. With your mind and body working together, you can focus and move forward.

Help Your Children Focus Too

Adults are not the only ones whose performance is affected by visual clutter. Researchers at Carnegie Mellon University investigated whether the number of displays in children's classrooms affected children's ability to maintain focused attention during instruction and to learn the lesson content.

Kindergartners were placed in different laboratory classrooms with varying degrees of decoration. The results showed that children were more distracted in the highly decorated environments. They spent more time off task and demonstrated smaller learning gains than when the decorations were removed.

It's no surprise that the same thing happens at home. The more cluttered spaces are in which your children play or do their schoolwork, the more difficult it can be for them to focus.

When your children have clutter-free spaces in the home to do schoolwork, they can focus better on the task to be done. Additionally, when children are certain where their studying tools or toys go, because you have an effective organizational system, it will be easier for them to put their things away when they are finished using them.

CLIENT CHRONICAL: PAPERWORK IN CLEAR VIEW

I had a client, we will call her Monica, who hired me to help her review and declutter the paper in her home filing cabinets. She had several filing cabinet drawers filled with papers.

Monica shared with me that she really hated to file and organize papers. I told her I felt the same way, and it's why I'm very discerning about what actually makes it into a file. My goal is to use my physical files for storing important documents like insurance policies, certificates, and so on, rather than a place to hold reference materials. This is because reference materials like product manuals and school lunch options and city recycling schedules can easily be found online.

A lightbulb went on for her when she realized that she was saving some reference materials out of habit. She had a huge stack of home product manuals and hadn't ever referenced them. If she had a problem with a TV or a vacuum or something similar, she usually looked up information online or called someone to repair it.

Within a few hours, we whittled down her papers from five filing cabinet drawers to two. And because the volume was so much less and the system had been simplified, she had a clear picture of what she had and has been easily able to maintain the system ever since.

Save Time

Forgetting stuff happens to everyone. We've all spent time looking for car keys or a mobile phone. Whatever the reason, we all forget where we put stuff, but some of us forget more than others and clutter plays a part.

According to a survey released by Pixie, a location app for iPhones, Americans spend over five minutes every time they misplace something. An average of 2.5 days a year are spent looking for misplaced stuff. People are also late to work or school (60 percent in the study), miss appointments or meetings (49 percent in the study), or even miss a flight, train, or bus (22 percent in the study) because they can't find what they were looking for on time.

When you declutter holistically, you will open up space in your home, space in your calendar, and space in your mind. Doing this allows you to spend more time living and less time rushing and managing.

Save Money

There is a cost to all of your clutter. If you've ever bought something to re-place something you think you've lost, but then found again, you know that is money you could have spent elsewhere.

Having less clutter can save you money in even larger ways. One of my clients, whom we'll call Roxanne, lived in a two-story home, but the basement was unusable because it was completely filled with clutter. The family had so much clutter in the basement that they had discussed buying a new home in order to get more space. To stay in the same neighborhood with a larger-sized home, they were facing a potential $50,000 to $100,000 investment.

The more we buy, the more space we need to store it. Families are buying larger homes to hold all of their stuff, which cost more money. According to the United States Census, the median-sized house has increased in size by almost 1,000 square feet (93 m^2) since 1973, while the average amount of living space per person in that same time has nearly doubled.

● *When you know and maintain what you have, you will spend less money replacing items.*

Where to Start

The months before my husband and I were first-time parents, we prepared. We read books on parenting, we watched videos on parenting, we took classes on parenting, and we prepared our house for a new baby in every way. We thought we were completely ready for our new baby to come—until she arrived jaundiced and colicky.

To say we were overwhelmed was putting it lightly. Even with all of the preparation, we missed the big picture. We were so focused on all of the details of getting the stuff we needed like diapers and clothes and toys, we didn't stop to consider how we'd like to teach and lead our children.

I realized this after reading a book about getting our colicky baby to sleep through the night. We'd hoped to learn tips and tricks we needed to get some sleep, like holding our baby or feeding her something special, but the author started with something simpler and more profound:

Start as you mean to go on.

I was blown away. In the midst of all of the chaos of crying and tummy aches and dirty laundry and failed attempts at breastfeeding, we were being asked to take a chill pill and consider the bigger picture. Absolutely brilliant.

The reason it was so brilliant is it helped us see that our colic problem was small compared to all the years we would spend with our daughter. If we used a couple seemingly simple solutions to just get her to stop crying, we might create bigger problems down the road. The same principle holds true when feeling overwhelmed with the clutter—the clutter in your house, the clutter on your calendar, and the clutter in your mind.

When things get overwhelming and out of control, we need to look up. We need to take a deep breath, expand our thinking, and explore what's possible. Then we can begin to move forward with a clear head and a clear direction.

And that is exactly what we're going to do next.

Holistically decluttering your life is similar to opening a door to a fresh new day.

Look at the Whole Picture

I worked with a family who had struggled with clutter for as far back as they could remember. The clutter restricted what they could do as a family as well as whom they would ask to come to their home. I could feel the heavy burden the clutter had on their family when I walked into the home.

When I asked the family what they wanted to get out of the whole house decluttering, the eldest boy said that he'd like to be able to have a friend come over. I asked if he'd had friends over in the past, and he told me that he had not because it was too messy at his house.

So off we went into the journey—one box, cupboard, and dresser at a time. There was a lot to get through, but we dug and dug. When I could see the family getting tired or frustrated, I got them to tell me again what they'd hoped their hard work would do for them as a family. I reminded them that they would be able to host events, enjoy each other's company, and no longer feel the burden of the clutter.

It was those reminders to look at the whole picture of the life they had envisioned that was the fuel they needed to get them to the end of the journey. And when it was done, friends and family could easily come over and enjoy the new space together.

It takes *courage*
to follow your heart,
so dig deep and
listen to
what it's telling you.

How to Envision Your Desired Life

Diving straight into a large decluttering effort without having a clear picture of the life you're trying to create will make the journey more difficult. Sure, you'll start out strong, just like most people do when starting something new, like a New Year's resolution. But a bigger vision helps you when you've hit the murky middle.

The murky middle is the place that lives right in between huge amounts of progress and a long road ahead. Your vision is like a headlamp when the road gets dark: You can turn your vision on, and it will illuminate the next few steps toward the finish line up ahead. But you likely can't see the finish line yet.

Writing down your vision also makes it more likely that you'll achieve it. According to a study conducted by Dr. Gail Matthews, a psychology professor at the Dominican University in California, you are 42 percent more likely to achieve your goals and dreams simply by writing them down. So, on the following pages, I'm inviting you to do just that.

● *Envisioning the path you want to follow is worth the time and effort.*

My Desired Life

(Current + Future)

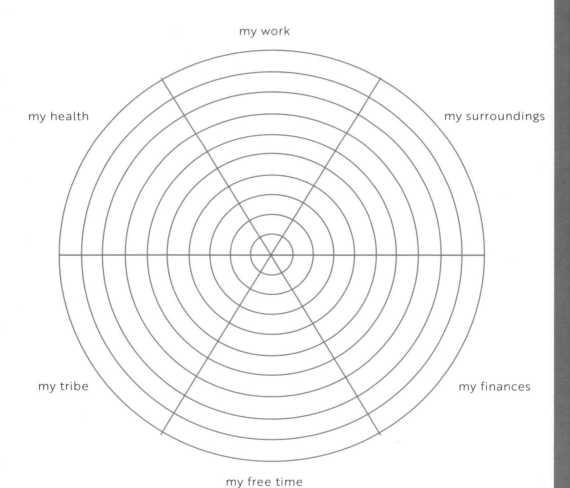

my work

my health

my surroundings

my tribe

my finances

my free time

Step 1: My Desired Life Wheel Assessment

The first step is to complete the wheel assessment at left and reflect on how you visualize your life in various categories. Before you get started, I recommend you grab a quiet spot, a cup of coffee or tea, and a handful of colored pencils, crayons, or markers. You may want to fill this out with family members or by yourself. Once you are ready, rate your current life in each area from 1 to 10 by shading that number of rings on the chart starting at the center and working out. Then, set a goal for where you would like to see your life in the future by making a small mark at each goal line on the chart.

Definitions

My work

The word "work" is defined by you. Work might be going to a 9-to-5 office job every day, staying at home caring for your children, volunteering your time, or attending school or classes. However you define work, that is what you should reflect on as you complete this section of the wheel.

My surroundings

When you think about surroundings, consider where you most often spend your time. This might be your home or your office or your car. Think about how you feel in the place where you spend most of your time as you complete this section of the wheel.

My finances

Your finances are both what you earn and what you spend, so ponder how you feel about your finances holistically when evaluating this aspect of your life. Reflect on where you have had both financial success and opportunity as you complete this section of the wheel.

My free time

Free time might be when you finally get a minute to yourself, or maybe it's when you are in community with others. However you define free time, contemplate that as you complete this section of the wheel.

My tribe

The people who influence, support, and have fun with you in your life's journey are your tribe. And while the size of a tribe is different for everyone, your tribe likely consists of your closest family members and friends. Think broadly about tribe as you complete this section of the wheel.

My health

Consider how you keep your body physically and mentally healthy when reflecting on this section of your life.

When you're finished with the My Desired Life wheel, move on to Step 2: My Desired Life Goals (page 45).

My Desired Life Goals

	my goal	actions to get there
my work		
my surroundings		
my finances		
my free time		
my tribe		
my health		

Step 2: My Desired Life Goals

Now it's time to create goals for achieving your desired life in each of the six areas. Write your goals so they are clear and include a date. For example, a goal you might write for your surroundings is to declutter your entire home in the next three months. Once you have your goals written down, write down three concrete action steps to get you there.

Chapters 1 and 2 Checklist

☐ **Embrace the truth that you can change.** Sometimes it can feel as if there is no hope for change because you've been doing things one way for such a long time. The reality is, however, that when you are committed to and focused on change, you can change your behavior. And often, that change can be profound and life altering if you set your sights high enough.

☐ **Consider the three dimensions of clutter in your life.** The three dimensions of clutter—physical, time, and mental—show up differently for everyone. Take the time during this holistic decluttering journey to consider how each of these dimensions shows up in your life.

☐ **Look for the root cause of clutter in each dimension.** Once you have gained more awareness of how each of the three clutter dimensions is showing up in your life, dig deeply into each of the dimensions and see if you can find the root cause of the challenge in each area. Once you find the root, you can really make changes to decrease the stronghold that dimension of clutter has on your life.

☐ **Envision your desired life.** Creating a vision of how your most desired life looks in the future provides you with a north star to continue to look up to as you move along the journey. Without a vision of how you'd like your life to be in the future, it will be difficult for you to make it all the way through the difficult parts of the journey.

☐ **Create your desired life goals.** Having a vision is the first step, but putting goals in place to help you reach the vision is when you will gain traction and move closer to reaching your most desired life.

DECLUTTERING YOUR HOME

Decluttering your home is like meditation for your nervous system.

Most homes are not always picture perfect and clutter free, nor do they need to be. But when a home goes beyond a small amount of daily clutter that is easily managed, the clutter can become a real challenge and can get in the way of your living your most desired life.

When your home is filled with too much clutter, too much dirty laundry, too many unfinished projects, or too many dirty dishes, it can trigger anxiety and stress. This is why decluttering your home is the foundation to holistic decluttering. Getting your home free of clutter opens the door for a larger personal transformation.

When I was young, I always dreamed of having my own home. I was excited thinking of being on my own, but a bigger desire for me was to create a place where I could express my personal style. After moving several times in two decades, I've had several opportunities to creatively express my personal style and give purpose to my homes. What I've learned through trial (and a lot of error) is that the clearer the vision for the purpose of my home was in my mind, the easier it was for me to bring that vision to life.

Consider this as you begin reading this chapter: Our homes provide us with more than just a roof over our heads. A home can be a safe place where you can explore and create whatever your imagination desires. A home can be a place where you get inspired, a place where you enjoy spending time with family and friends, a place where you can heal when you're sick, and a place to explore new passions.

Before you dig into the details of how to declutter your home, take time to set your course. When you are intentional about what you are trying to create in your home, the process of bringing that vision to life can be transformative.

- *Sometimes, less is more in home décor. Creating a curated space can showcase the pieces you love most.*

Setting Intention Rather Than a Goal

Before I work with clients, I ask them to share their visions for their homes and their intentions before starting the decluttering journey. I do this, in part, so I know what they are trying to create and how I can help them stay true to those desires.

Sometimes, getting clear on intention is hard because it gets confused with setting a goal. Think of it this way: Goals are focused on a set destination of what we want to achieve in the future, while intentions are focused on the present moment and how we want to feel during the journey. Furthermore, goals are something you hope to achieve, but may fall short of, while intentions are something you plan to do regardless. Goals often come from the mind alone, while intentions come from your spirit (mind and body) and are about an inner relationship you have with yourself.

Let's look at an example to illustrate the difference. Let's say you set a goal to run a marathon. This goal would lead you to train your body to run longer and longer distances until you are able to run all 26.2 miles (42.2 km) in one run. On the other hand, a related intention might be to improve your health and physical fitness. Failing to run a marathon may mean you did not meet your goal, but by training, you would have followed your intention.

Goals are wonderful tools to help you achieve great things, but they can also bring on anxiety if you get too focused on how you are (or are not) getting to the goal. An intention offers you the opportunity to be your best at any given moment along the journey since it's an internal dialogue with your soul. Simply put, an intention gives credit to the journey, while a goal only gives credit to the achievement.

Now that you know the difference, let's dig into setting intention for your journey.

● *Give yourself the gift of a quiet space when setting your intention. The quiet space will help you hear the call of your soul.*

How to Set an Intention

There are many different ways to set an intention. For this exercise, you will follow three steps.

1. Find a quiet space
Find a quiet space where you know you will be uninterrupted for thirty minutes or more. Carve out enough time to give yourself the space you will need to listen to your inner voice.

2. Listen to your heart
As you sit in your quiet space, imagine your highest desire for your life. Imagine yourself already living that life and realigning what it feels like to be there. Reflect on the questions below to dig deeper into your vision.

- Where are you and what does the space around you look like?
- How does the space around you feel?
- What is happening around you?
- What are you doing?
- How do *you* feel?
- Who are you sharing time with?
- What have you let go of?

3. Set your intention
As you sit and reflect on each question, write down your answer when you feel your heart and mind are in agreement. Give yourself enough time to reflect on each question, but don't overthink it. There are no wrong answers. Then complete the Intention Statement at right.

Intention Statement

My name is _____ , and it is my intention to live

a _____ , _____ ,

and _____ life. I am grateful for

_____ and _____ .

I know I'm the author of my life based on the choices I make each day and how

I think and act toward myself and others. To create my most desired life, I intend

to _____ and _____ and

to feel _____ and _____

along the journey.

It is my intent to attract _____ and

_____ into my life while letting go of

_____ and _____ .

I know things will not always go as I hope or plan, so I will be compassionate

to myself by _____ when things go sideways.

It is my intention to nurture relationships with _____

and _____ .

_____

(signature)

Embracing a helpful mindset—

one that is decisive, kind,

and guilt-free—

is essential

as you embark on your

holistic decluttering *journey*.

Embrace a Helpful Mindset

When you declutter your home, you will have an internal dialogue with yourself. You will be reviewing items you've spent your money on as well as items others have spent their money on and have given to you. For that reason, everything you touch is likely to strike up a thought in your mind and possibly an emotion in your body—positive, negative, or neutral.

Because your emotions can become overpowering, they have the ability to get in the way of finishing your journey. That is why it's important to embrace a helpful mindset before you start the journey. I would describe a helpful mindset as decisive, kind, and guilt-free. You can try to declutter with only one of these elements, but you may not have as much success as when you harness the power of using them all.

Be Decisive

Decluttering any space requires you to make a lot of decisions, which is why being decisive is so critical. But often, being decisive is easier said than done. And it's not an all-or-nothing thing! I've worked with clients who were very decisive in some areas of decluttering only to have extreme difficulties in other areas.

There is no way an outsider can predict what you will have a difficult time with when it comes to making decisions because it's so personal. What I can tell you from experience is that the best way to be decisive is to make decisions as either "yes" or "no" rather than allowing a "maybe."

When my clients have a hard time deciding, they often ask me if they could put an item into the middle "maybe" category. I sometimes allow it for part of the session, but I will come back to the item before I leave and ask them to make a firm yes-or-no decision. Why? Because if they are not ready to let it go, then they should decide to joyfully keep it. They shouldn't relegate it to a place of perpetual indecision.

Use Joy and Service to Help You Decide

Now that we know why it's important to be decisive in decluttering, let me share why I think joy and service are the two most helpful filters to guide you through tough decisions.

One of the lessons I learned while traning in the KonMari method of decluttering was that joy is the filter upon which all decisions should be made. In practice, this means that you would ask yourself if an item brings you joy when you are looking at it. If the answer is yes, you would keep it. If the answer is no, it would be discarded.

In many circumstances, the joy filter is strong enough for clients to make a decision. Yet I have found there are times when the joy-only filter is not strong enough to help guide a decision. This is usually the case with extremely practical items and with clients who are needing to downsize. When this occurs, adding the second filter of service comes in handy.

In the case of the extremely practical items, my clients will say the "[fill-in-the-blank boring item] gives me no joy at all, but I still need it." That's when evaluating its service can come in handy. If you use the filter of how well it is serving a need, sometimes that can help nudge you to a decision. If you find an item that is necessary but not filling a need, you can still discard it.

For example, I had a client who told me that her spatula did not bring her any joy, but she needed it. When I asked her what needed to change in order for it to be both practical and joy filling, she said that she would prefer it was a dark color so it wouldn't turn red when used on red-sauced food. When I asked her if she was open to letting it go in order to find one that would be of good service and provide joy, she was excited to find that item and joyfully let go of the one that didn't bring her joy.

If you are downsizing and haven't decluttered in many years (or decades), you might find that more items bring you joy than will comfortably fit into the new space. When that is the case, the second filter of service is extremely important.

I had a client who knew she needed to downsize, but when we went through her things, so many brought her joy. Unfortunately, the volume was more than her space would allow. You might be in a similar situation. If so, it's best to use the service filter. Consider how will it serve you to have so much in your new space that you cannot comfortably move around and enjoy the space.

Decluttering by category is helpful because it helps you see if you have a volume issue—even if all of the items spark joy. A client of mine, whom we will call Sandy, was a teacher and loved office supplies. They brought her a lot of joy. Unfortunately, the volume was too large for the new space, and even in the current space, it was making things difficult to find.

We gathered her supplies and had her sort through small subcategories of items so she could see the volume. When she saw she owned eight tape dispensers, she couldn't believe it and

● *Even utilitarian items like kitchen utensils can be curated.*

said goodbye to six. Then she saw she had over thirty sewing scissors and was able to reduce the volume by half. When she saw she had forty or fifty pads of sticky notes, it became clear that even though those items did bring her joy, they were not serving her well because they were getting in the way of her enjoying her life and moving on.

Keep in mind that there is no right or wrong way to make a decision when decluttering. The most important thing is that you can arrive at a decision for every item and then move on.

● *Everyone makes mistakes and is learning, so be kind to yourself as you take on new experiences and knowledge.*

Use a Kind and Compassionate Internal Voice

Many of us use a harsh, condemning, negative voice when talking to ourselves internally. We often do this when we think we've done something wrong or wished we could get a do-over on a decision we've made. This comes up a lot when decluttering because we are evaluating many past decisions.

The reality is that no one is perfect. We've all made purchases we regret, but that doesn't mean we need to be unkind to ourselves because of that decision.

What is more helpful is that you look at your past purchases as transactions and learn lessons from them. In time, you will learn more about yourself and your preferences and will be able to be more intentional as you move forward rather than getting upset with yourself for something that is in the past. See the difference a little compassion can make by reviewing the table at right.

Finding Your Compassionate Voice

Critical Voice Says	Compassionate Voice Says
• You're not good/smart/ attractive enough.	• Your worth is inherent and not determined by approval or acceptance from others.
• You're not likable.	• You're learning how to accept and receive love.
• You're not allowed to make mistakes.	• Everyone makes mistakes. It's part of our imperfect being.
• Your voice doesn't matter.	• The world needs to hear what you have to say.
• You're weak.	• You're getting stronger.

CLIENT CHRONICAL: BAD DECISION BOXES

I once helped a college student and her mother, let's call them Jenna and Jane, declutter and organize every inch of their large three-story home. It was going to take six to eight days to finish the entire project. After several days with the family, we focused on Jenna's room, where we found many empty boxes from a popular makeup line.

When I first grabbed all of the boxes, probably around fifty, I thought this was going to be a simple exercise in breaking down the boxes and putting them into the recycling. It was not.

At first, Jenna said she would like to repurpose the boxes for our organizing. I liked the idea, but I knew we wouldn't need that many. She got it down to twenty of the best ones. As the decluttering session went along, it became obvious that we wouldn't need to use any of the boxes for organizing. At that point, I asked Jenna if we could recycle the remaining boxes and the truth came out.

She was actually holding onto the boxes as a visual reminder of what she called "bad decisions." She had spent a lot of her money on the makeup that had been in the boxes. She said she was keeping the boxes as a reminder of those bad decisions so she would never make them again. I reminded her that life is a series of learning moments and that no one is perfect. I asked her how she felt when she looked at the boxes, and she said that they made her feel bad and guilty.

She was not able to let go of the boxes before I left, but my heart was delighted when I received a text from her later that she'd made the decision to recycle them all because she had learned the lesson from our session.

Let Go of Guilt

Guilt is a strong emotion. At the most basic cognitive level, guilt is an emotion we experience because we're convinced we've caused someone harm. I see most guilt come up not because my clients have actually caused someone harm but because they believe their actions might cause someone harm in the future.

Take, for example, a client's kitchen declutter. We pulled every non-food item out of the cupboards and put them onto the counters. We moved similar items together, and then I guided my client through each subcategory of items—dishes, glasses, platters, silverware, cooking tools, pots and pans, and so on—and asked her to make a decision about each item.

As she started making decisions about what she wanted to keep, the discard pile started to grow. I often ask my clients to reflect on the discard pile to see what they can learn from it. When I asked the client to reflect on the pile, she said two things. First, she didn't realize how much she disliked the color red. And second, she noticed that she had been holding onto a lot of items that had been gifted to her by her mother.

This is not an uncommon scenario. Gifts can be the kryptonite of decluttering. I've watched well-reasoning, well-educated adults become paralyzed when looking at an old gift from a relative or a friend. When I ask them to tell me the origination story along with questions like: "Do you love it?" or "Does it bring you joy?" I hear, "It was a gift," followed quickly by, "No, I don't like it, but it was a gift so I should keep it," or, "My mom/dad/whoever would be hurt if I didn't keep it." More than once, I've even heard, "I'll get rid of it when so-and-so dies."

Gift guilt is an emotion that can feel heavy. It is obvious to me when a client holds a gift they don't want to keep. When people hold a gift in their hands that their hearts treasure, their faces light up, and the decision to keep it is made quickly.

I encourage my clients to be true to their hearts and empower themselves to make decisions that are right for them at that time. If that means saying thank you for the gift and joyfully discarding it, then so be it.

It is very likely that there is a conversation that needs to happen around a gift that triggers fear. It may seem easier to keep a gift you don't like rather than to have a heart-to-heart with someone to say, "Thank you, but my tastes have changed so I no longer have the item." Trust me, I do know this is difficult. But when we are talking about a full-scale transformation, it means you will likely go through some old wounds. Think of it as part of the journey.

How to Declutter Your Home

When you decide to declutter your entire home, get ready for a marathon and not a sprint. Unlike what some reality TV shows might have you believe, decluttering an entire home in a weekend is not realistic. There are a lot of factors that go into how long it will take to declutter your entire home, including how much clutter you have, your emotional state, and other time commitments.

Set a Timeline

I recommend you declutter everything in your home in a set timeframe. There is no need to pressure yourself to finish in one weekend, but it is important to set a general timeframe. I generally recommend decluttering to be focused in one season, so approximately three to four months.

What's important is to choose a timeframe that is aspirational, yet achievable. You want to allow enough time so you can be thorough in your review of all of your items and, therefore, be successful, but not so much time that it becomes a never-ending project.

A timeline also helps hold you accountable. You will be able to use your momentum from each mini success in your timeline to get you to the finish line. (On the other hand, the "starting and stopping without a finish line" approach can be almost more frustrating than never starting at all.)

If there is a motivating event in your life (e.g., you are hosting a family reunion in about a month), that can add to the motivation to finish the declutter. Use that to your advantage, if possible.

● *Whether you dream of a neatly organized pantry or a top-to-bottom declutter of the kitchen, setting a timeline will help you keep a finish line in sight.*

One of my clients, we'll call her Caryn, learned that her grown daughter, who had been living in a different state, needed to move back home with her fiancé for several months while they looked for a new home. Caryn had been thinking of decluttering for some time, but this life event, which was only four months away, gave her the kick she needed to get focused and make a change.

Initially, her hope was to have a space where her daughter and her fiancé could live comfortably. After a few sessions, she realized the amount of joy that decluttering and putting her house in order had given her was an even greater gift. She completed her whole house decluttering journey and felt both emotionally and physically ready to welcome her daughter and her daughter's fiancé into a home she is proud of.

If you don't have a special event in your future, you can simply create one as a starting point. There is nothing like having an event you are hosting to motivate yourself to declutter.

Declutter by Category

There are many different schools of thought on how to start the decluttering process. I have learned that the easiest way to declutter is to go one category at a time. This means, instead of choosing a room to declutter, you choose a category. As an example, we'll look at clothes.

- You first gather up clothes from every place you have them in your home. That means you would combine the clothes from your closet, your dressers, your hall closets, your spare bedrooms, your bins in the basement, and so on.

- Once you have all of your clothes in one place, look at each item one by one and determine if you want to keep it. If the volume of items you are looking at feels too large and is overwhelming, pull together a subcategory of like items (e.g., pants) and go through one subcategory at a time.

Focus Your Mind on the "Keeps"

Because decluttering is often thought of as synonymous with letting go, you might worry you will have to let go of items you are attached to. Sometimes clients express concern that I might "make them" get rid of things they want to keep. However, forceful mandates, or alternately shame and guilt, are not the best tools to use when decluttering. I like to have my clients focus less on what they are getting rid of and instead turn their focus to what they are going to keep.

I tell my clients: Your job is simple. You are going to look at everything you own, and you are going to pick out the stuff you want to keep. That's it. When you focus your mind on what you want to keep, your mind can pivot and become focused on curating. Just like an art collector who is choosing which pieces to put on display in an art gallery, you are choosing the items you wish to put on display and use in your home. You are giving those items a home and a purpose. Being selective is part of the process, and it makes it very obvious which items no longer work.

Express Gratitude

Because emotion can surface when decluttering, I believe it's important to express your gratitude throughout the process. Expressing gratitude for the service or the lesson an item had in our lives lets us complete the cycle of ownership.

This expression of gratitude doesn't need to be a long or dramatic process, just a simple thank you will do. It can be an internal reflection of gratitude or one that is expressed verbally.

We do not need to be afraid of letting go of an item from our past. By letting go of something we no longer love or that no longer provides us service, we are opening ourselves up for what is next.

Save Sentimental Items for Last

Ever start decluttering a drawer and find yourself lost in a picture from high school and then never finish decluttering the drawer? Sentimental items is often the hardest category to declutter. Doing the sentimental category last allows you to hone your decision-making skills and relieves you from the weight of all of the other categories.

One of my clients, whom I'll call Grace, had lost her son Jack to cancer ten years before she called me for help. When I toured the home, we stopped by Jack's room, and it was exactly as it had been when he passed. I could feel the grief as I stood with Grace looking into Jack's room. I told her that we would get to sorting through Jack's things during the process, but it would be the final step.

We had a lot to declutter over the course of our many days together. When it was time to sort through Jack's old clothes, even I was a little nervous. We were near the end of a session, so I asked if she felt ready to do it or if she wanted to wait. She said she was ready, so we moved forward.

With me kneeling on the floor with a bag of clothes and Grace kneeling across from me, I pulled out each piece of clothing one at a time. Tears immediately started to stream down Grace's face and then down mine. I didn't know Jack personally, but I had learned so much about him during my time with Grace that I felt as if I knew him too. I reminded my client about the importance of expressing gratitude and saying goodbye. She clung to each shirt for a moment and said goodbye. It was one of the most deeply emotional experiences I've had while decluttering. To watch this mother keep her little boy in her heart, but also make space for what was to come next in her life was incredible.

When we were finished going through all of the clothes, my client said that sorting through the clothes was easier than she had imagined for two reasons. First, she'd already accomplished so much in our time together that she hadn't believed she could. And second, her heart felt at peace because we took the time to sit in gratitude and say goodbye.

Had we decluttered the clothing any earlier in the process, we might not have been as successful. Resist the urge to dig into letters and photos on day one. Give yourself time to practice. This will make working through sentimental items easier and more joyful.

● *Sentimental items can present roadblocks. There is nothing wrong with saving them until after the easy wins.*

● *Preparing your space with baskets or bags before you declutter will help speed along the process once you get going.*

Discarding

Discarding, which is the act of getting rid of an item from your home, is a very important step in the decluttering process because it opens up your living spaces. It's helpful for you to prepare bags, baskets, or bins with labels on them for the different categories of discards: sell, donate, trash, and recycle.

Then, as you begin to make your decisions, you have a place for your discards to go. Once you are finished decluttering a category, it is important to remove the discards from your house that same day. Leaving piles of discards throughout the house is simply adding more clutter.

I've had many people tell me that doing the work to actually get rid of the things they don't want is one of the hardest steps. Many have confessed to having had bags of items for donation sitting in their cars for weeks. If this sounds like you, then ask for help from a friend and see if they can be your discard buddy. They can accompany you or hold you accountable for getting the items you are saying goodbye to out of your space.

Sell

If you want to turn your clutter into cash, there are different ways to do that, but they require some work on your part. The three primary ways to sell your items are:

- consignment
- a digital marketplace or app
- a garage or yard sale

When you give an item to a consignment store, it will pay you a portion of what it makes on the item. The typical process is to find a consignment store near your home and bring your items to the store.

If consignment isn't your cup of tea, there are many online marketplaces and apps where you can sell your unwanted items quickly. Some options require you to pay a fee, while others let you sell your unwanted items for free. A buyer can come to your home to pick up the item, or you can arrange everything through the mail. The options are endless and constantly changing.

If neither of those ways to sell appeals to you, there is always the tried-and-true garage or yard sale where you open up your garage or home and set out your items to sell. While this was once a very popular way to sell items, it has become less frequent given all of the new choices.

Donate

If you don't need to turn your clutter into cash, donating is a wonderful option because there is so much need in the world. Choosing to sell your items adds more to-dos to the already large to-do list, so I often encourage my clients to consider donating if they have the means to do so.

There are many ways to donate to people in your local community and around the world. You can donate to large organizations or to countless nonprofits, churches, thrift stores, and organizations in your community.

Recycle

It does take more time to responsibly dispose of some household items, but part of the responsibility of owning things is to take care of them through their entire life cycle. I've also learned that not taking the time to recycle properly can actually do more harm than good in the long run. Glass and paper products are the easiest items to recycle, and nearly all of the items can be used again.

Plastics, electronics, and hazardous waste items take a bit of research to determine the best way to dispose of them, but it's useful information. Most cities have a resource to help residents learn how to dispose of hazardous waste items locally. Some items are free to dispose of, while other items have a fee. Some stores can take electronic items for recycling as well. Take the time to find a local facility near you so you know what to do when the time comes.

Trash

While a zero-waste home is a wonderful goal, the reality is that there will always be a need for some items to be thrown away during a decluttering marathon.

Items that might end up in the trash bag include dried-up paint cans, non-recyclable plastics, rusted objects, carpeting, and broken household items that cannot be recycled.

I recommend that you estimate how much trash you think you will have before you get started. If you're downsizing and decluttering 40 years of items, a dumpster might be the best solution for your trash. On the other hand, if you think that your weekly trash service will be enough to hold all of your trash, then no need to make other arrangements.

Decluttering Your Home Checklist

☐ **Embrace a helpful mindset.** A helpful mindset is being decisive, kind, and guilt free. Embracing this type of mindset will take you far in your decluttering journey and will allow you to move through an important phase of the process with ease.

☐ **Set a timeline.** The initial whole home decluttering effort should have clear start and end dates. Without a clear end date, you could be left with a never-ending project on your hands.

☐ **Declutter by category.** Sorting through all of your things by category, rather than by room, helps you compare and contrast the items within each category and makes it easier for you to make clear decisions.

☐ **Focus on the "keeps."** Focusing your mind on what items you choose to keep as you are decluttering is a positive way to sort through your things. Doing so allows you to search out items you love rather than items you don't. The items you don't want to keep will clearly not belong with the others.

☐ **Discard with intention.** Using intention as you discard the items you no longer wish to keep is a meaningful end to the life cycle of your things. By putting as much care into the end of the usefulness of something you've owned is just as important as the care you gave it when it was new.

ORGANIZING YOUR HOME

Organizing isn't the goal; simplifying your life is.

Imagine for a moment that your home is a place where everything you see is something you love. Imagine that all of those items you love are put away, leaving your home free of clutter, and it is now a space that can simply be enjoyed.

When you live in an organized home, it feels more peaceful. It feels like a calm sea rather than a roaring storm. As the mother of a teen and a tween, I know there are enough rough waters to navigate every day! I'm grateful when I can find strategies that add a little more peace in my life.

Living in an organized home is also easier. It's easier because you know what you have, you can find what you need when you need it, and you have systems in place that make putting things away after you use them less difficult. Knowing where everything in your home lives is an empowering feeling. It means you'll no longer rush around in the morning looking for your wallet or keys. You'll no longer get hit with a flash of anxiety when you're asked to supply an important piece of paper because you don't know where to begin looking for it.

In the event you think home organization is the pursuit of perfection, let me be clear: It's not. As a recovering perfectionist, I have plenty of personal examples when I've gone too far in the pursuit of excellence. More times than I'd like to admit, I've overdone something in the pursuit of perfect and, in doing so, paid a price for it. (Usually that price was stolen joy and exhaustion.) The real goal of organizing your home is to simplify your life so you will be able to enjoy it more.

That said, it's also important to realize that keeping a home organized is not a spectator sport. You will need to do work to get your home organized and additional work to keep it organized, but the reward is worth it. When you have a home that is decluttered and organized, it has the power to take your everyday life and transform it.

In this chapter, we will dig into more detail on how to organize your home so you will begin to feel the peace and ease described earlier. If that sounds good to you, keep reading.

- *Reach for something and it's right where you left it: That's the beauty of organized spaces.*

How to Organize Your Home

Organizing is actually quite simple, yet it can seem challenging if you've never learned the basic principles shared in detail in the pages that follow. In this chapter, we will first dig into six big concepts of organizing that can be applied to any space. Then, we will examine some of the most challenging spaces to organize in a home, which include the kitchen and pantry, clothing storage, bathrooms, laundry, and toys. My hope is that, by the end, you will feel better prepared to take on the challenge of organizing your own home and begin to transform it one step at a time.

Many of my clients found that learning how to organize their homes inspired confidence and motivated them to take on the task. For some, though, it might not be that simple. After all, creating an organizational system from scratch doesn't come naturally to everyone. Many people have a powerful and sometimes negative memory of a time when they struggled to organize a particular room or space. If this is you, don't feel bad. There is no shame in having to ask a friend for help or to hire a professional organizer. Everyone's path to creating and maintaining an organized home is unique.

Assign a "Home" for Everything

The golden rule of organizing is to assign a home within your house for everything you own. Assigning a home means you will designate one place in your house where an item (or subcategory of like items) lives. Not having ever assigned a home to certain items can be the underlying problem for why a space is disorganized. If this rings true for you, then read on.

When you assign a home for everything you own, it makes it easier for you to find what you need when you need it. Having a home for everything is helpful not only when there is more than one person living in a space but also if you live alone. When you live alone, the burden of all of the housework and upkeep lands on you, so having strategies to simplify your day to day is important.

Designating a "home" for everything you own makes it easier to find what you need when you need it.

Here are some tips for deciding where your things should live.

Store active items in active spaces.
All homes have items and spaces used more often than others. If an item or space is used on a daily or weekly basis, it is an active item or space. The entryway, kitchen, and bathroom are examples of active spaces. Storing active items in the active spaces makes it easier for you to use those spaces effectively.

Store storage items in storage spaces.
Inactive or less-used items are best stored in storage spaces outside of the active spaces of a home. An example of this is storing holiday decorations in plastic bins on shelves in the basement or garage.

Store active items in close proximity to their use.
In an active space, it is ideal for the active items to be stored in close proximity to where they will be used. An example of this is storing a toothbrush in the bathroom medicine cabinet. Another example might be storing oils and spices where you prepare meals in the kitchen rather than having them far away in the pantry.

Try keeping counters clear.
The more items you need to move in order to clean, the less likely you will be to clean the space. This is why it is important to store as little as possible on countertops. It is much easier to store items within reach of the countertop, but not on the countertop, so you are able to clean the space easily. Space constraints sometimes mean that items have to be stored on a countertop, but consider it a last resort.

Store kid and pet items with care.
Both kids and pets have specific needs to consider when you are selecting where to store items in your home. Consider whether you want your children and/or your pets to be able to reach the items. Storing items at kids' level is ideal when you want them to be able to get them out and put them back on their own, but out of reach is best for items that can be harmful to kids or pets.

Store Like with Like

Once you've decided what items will go into active spaces and what items will go into storage spaces, it's important to organize similar items together. This concept is more intuitive for some categories than for others.

For example, in most homes I visit, my clients store plates with plates in the kitchen cupboard, but they might not put pasta with pasta in the pantry. By putting like items with like items throughout your home, you are more easily able to see the volume of what you own.

When you spread categories of items throughout the home it becomes more difficult to inventory what you have, which often leads to purchasing items you don't need.

Subcategorize into Manageable Categories

Sometimes the act of putting like with like gets challenging when you're not quite sure how big the category should be. For example, you could store all of your kid's toys in one large bin and it would be organized; but it likely wouldn't be an effective system unless your volume of toys is low. It is easier to find and use the toys if you divide the large category of toys into smaller, more manageable subcategories that make sense to you—like storing cars with cars, games with games, and dolls with dolls.

Breaking down the categories into smaller subcategories could take a little trial and error on your part. In some cases, you will want to break down the large subcategories into several smaller subcategories. Craft items are a good example of this. You could start by breaking down crafts into smaller subcategories like paper, stickers, glue, and paint. However, if you find that it isn't easy for you to keep the subcategories organized, it might require you to break a subcategory down even further. For example, instead of all paper being together, you might break it down into white paper, colored paper, and scrapbook paper.

The number of times you need to further divide a subcategory can usually be determined through experimentation. You might find you need to divide to a very small level in some categories and not in others.

Remove Store Packaging

The extra packaging that comes with many of the things we buy takes up a lot of space, so it's best to remove as much of that packaging as possible as soon as you get home from the store. Some examples of extra packaging include the cardboard box that holds the granola bars, the cardboard sleeve around a package of hummus, and even the large plastic bag that holds individual-sized bags of chips.

If you remove all of the excess packaging when you unpack items from the store, you will take all of the packaging to the recycling and garbage at one time. This might not seem like a major win until you realize you are not having to put things into the recycling throughout the day.

Finally, removing store packaging simplifies taking inventory because you are able to quickly see how much of something you have rather than be deceived by the size of the box. We've all been frustrated by an empty box of cereal or granola.

Divide Your Drawers

Drawer dividers are some of the hardest-working storage items available and work equally great in kitchens, bathrooms, and bedrooms. It is a very rare case where I wouldn't recommend a drawer divider of some sort for a drawer.

Drawer dividers allow you to break down the contents of a drawer into manageable subcategories, making it easy to find things when you need them and keeping them from getting jumbled with everything else in the drawer.

Label

Labeling is the final step to organizing any space. Labeling helps you and the people you live with know where things go without having to guess. The options for labels are endless and range from something as simple as using a marker to write directly on the bin or box to investing in a label-making machine.

My favorite label option is removable vinyl labels because they allow for a refined and finished look when organizing, yet they can also be easily removed when I need to change things from time to time.

How to Organize a Kitchen

Before I founded Neat Little Nest, I spent decades working alongside chefs in my corporate career. One of my longtime partners in food innovation was a chef named Mark Miller, who taught me a lot about preparing foods, cooking, and kitchen setups. Mise en place is a concept that I carried with me as I began to work with my clients as they organized their kitchens.

Mise en place is a culinary term for "putting in place" or "everything in its place." For chefs, it means having their ingredients measured, cut, peeled, sliced, and grated before they start cooking. Pans are prepared. Mixing bowls, tools, and equipment are set out. It allows the chef to quickly put a meal together.

Dividing a utensil drawer makes it easier to find what you're looking for.

When organizing a kitchen, the mise en place philosophy applies. Everything should have a clear and defined place. Doing this has many benefits including faster food prep, faster prep for grocery shopping, and the ability for all members of the household to participate in keeping it organized. These benefits all lead to decreasing mealtime stress.

There are a few steps to take when applying the mise en place philosophy to kitchen organization, so let's dive into them.

Divide the Kitchen into Zones

A good first step to organizing a kitchen is to divide the space into high-level zones. You can do this mentally or draw a quick sketch. Choose whichever option is most helpful to you.

The four primary zones I consider are the working triangle, the dishwashing/dishwasher area, the pantry (or cabinets designated for food storage), and the dining area.

- **Embrace a helpful mindset.** A helpful mindset is being decisive, kind, and guilt free. Embracing this type of mindset will take you far in your decluttering journey and will allow you to move through an important phase of the process with ease.

- **The working triangle,** also known as the kitchen triangle, was a theory developed in the early twentieth century that states that a kitchen has three main work areas and they should form a triangle. Those three main work areas are the sink, the refrigerator, and the stove.

- **The dishwashing/dishwasher** area includes the dishwasher (if you have one), the sink, the area under the sink, and the counter next to the sink. For this area to be useful, the sink and the counter need to be cleared off and available at every meal.

- **The pantry** is where nonperishable food is stored. The pantry might be a dedicated and separate space inside the kitchen, a set of kitchen cabinets, or a few shelves outside of the kitchen, depending on the design of your home.

- **The dining area** is wherever you sit down to eat. It might be a formal room with a large table, a table in the kitchen, or simply a counter with stools.

Once you have the kitchen divided into zones in your mind or sketched out on a piece of paper, it's time to consider what should go into each of these zones.

Determining What Goes Where

There are three main categories of items that go into a kitchen—items you use to cook, items you use to eat, and food. In order to have an organized kitchen, you need to determine where all of those items will go. What can make this task overwhelming is the sheer number of items used and stored in a kitchen. But, if you take it step by step, you will easily be able to decide what goes where and will have a well-organized kitchen in no time.

Let's start by looking at the items we use to cook and the items we use to eat, based on type of use and frequency of use.

Type of Use

	Items Used to Cook	Items Used to Eat
HIGH	The items you use most frequently when cooking should be placed inside the working triangle. These items include pots, pans, mixing bowls, knives, measuring tools, as well as ingredients such as oils, vinegars, and spices.	The items you use most frequently when eating should be placed closest to the dishwasher. These include plates, bowls, glasses, cups, cutlery, and serving items such as platters and napkins.
LOW	The items you use less frequently when cooking should be placed in less-accessible kitchen spaces or storage spaces. These items include seasonal cooking and baking tools as well as less-used specialty cooking items.	The items you use less frequently when eating should be placed in less-accessible kitchen spaces or storage spaces. These items include seasonal serving items as well as less-used specialty serving items.

FREQUENCY OF USE

As you can see on the chart above, when you look at all of the items in your kitchen based on those two dimensions, some clear recommendations emerge as to where the best place to store an item might be.

After you've decided where you will store the items used to cook and the items used to eat, you can decide where you would like to store the food. Usually food will either be stored in the refrigerator/freezer or on shelves inside kitchen cabinets or in a separate pantry.

CLIENT CHRONICAL: BUSY FAMILY KITCHEN

One of my clients, we'll call her Tiffany, was a mom with four children under the age of ten who had a very disorganized kitchen. She had some spaces where it was clear what lived there, but most of the spaces didn't have a system in place.

And without a system in place that she could teach her children to use, she was left trying to manage all of the spaces herself. As a result, she was frazzled and exhausted. In particular, it was difficult to see and to quickly access what was in the pantry.

When I saw the pantry, I told her that I thought her challenge was the lack of a clear system and that if we created one, she would be able to teach it to her kids. She was skeptical but agreed to move forward.

We pulled everything out and made a defined system using bins, labels, and decanting a lot of items into clear containers so she could easily see what she had. A few hours later, she had a transformed pantry and was thrilled, but she was still concerned that the family couldn't keep it that way. I said that they would have to do some maintenance, but if she showed the family and held them accountable for using the system, the pantry would be organized for years to come.

I'm happy to share that months after our visit, I checked in on the status of the pantry and it was almost exactly as we had left it. The kids actually enjoyed being able to see and find a snack quickly, and it became almost fun helping to put away groceries.

Organizing a Refrigerator

When hunger strikes, the last thing you want to do is rummage through your fridge or freezer, removing or pushing ingredients aside to get to what you need. For a variety of reasons (fewer trips to the grocery store, large families, teenage boys, etc.), many are tempted to overfill the refrigerator shelves and drawers. But this gets in the way of something more important: Your kitchen should be your happy place!

Organizing a refrigerator can be difficult because the items are likely to change from week to week, and the sizes of the items stored in the refrigerator vary. It is also a challenge because so many people go in and out of the refrigerator multiple times a day.

In this section, I will share strategies that have worked for my family as well as many Neat Little Nest clients. These are all strategies you can implement no matter the make or model of your appliance.

Before You Start, Clean it Out!

Before you can do any organizing, it's best to start with a clean slate. This means taking everything out at the same time. Scrub, wipe, and/or soak the shelves, the storage bins, the sidewalls, the sticky goop on bottles, the drip lines . . . you get the picture. Haven't looked at expiration dates in a while? When you have everything out of the fridge, check the dates and toss/recycle items that are past their prime.

Divide the Refrigerator into Zones

Once you've cleaned out the refrigerator, it's time to divide the refrigerator into zones, just like you did when dividing the kitchen. The refrigerator is home to many different categories of items, so there is potential for many zones. Below are the primary zones to consider:

- dairy
- meat
- fruit
- vegetables
- condiments
- leftovers

Creating zones in your refrigerator with plastic containers helps keep it tidy day to day.

Since every household is different, you might not have all of the zones mentioned or you might have them all plus a few more like a snack or lunch section for kids. In order to determine which zones you need, ask yourself a few questions.

- What consistent staple items need dedicated space in the refrigerator (fruit, eggs, milk, juice, veggies, meats, etc.)?

- Do you have kids? If yes, do you need a kid-friendly area where they can readily grab items and go?

- Do you typically have leftovers that require real estate? Do you/your family like a lot of sauces, syrups, condiments, or salad dressings?

Once you've determined the zones you want in your refrigerator, it's time to figure out where each zone goes.

Placement is Key for Food Quality and Freshness

Many people do not have a clear idea of where food is best stored in the refrigerator. Once I started my career as a professional organizer, I did some research and found out I was doing a lot of things that were not optimal for my food—and potentially my health! Here are guidelines to help you choose where to store your food.

- **Ready-to-eat foods,** such as dairy products, packaged foods, leftovers, cooked meats, and prepared salads, should be stashed on the top or middle shelves of your fridge. These should be covered well or kept in sealed containers to prevent contamination. Placement on the upper tiers, away from raw foods (greens, veggies, fruits, etc.), limits harmful bacteria from transferring from raw food to cooked food.

- **Leftovers** should be on one shelf, if possible, so they are not stashed throughout the refrigerator only to be found weeks later with mold on them.

- **Raw meat, poultry, and fish** should be placed in sealed containers on the lower-level shelves or drawers, which are typically the coolest. This placement also prevents them from touching or dripping onto other foods, which could cause cross-contamination.

- **Vegetables** are best stored in a different part of the fridge from fruit. This prevents them from ripening too fast. Most vegetables, like carrots, broccoli, and cabbage, are best stored in a plastic bag or container designed to keep them fresh in the fridge, while mushrooms are best stored in a paper bag.

- **Certain fruits, like berries and grapes,** are best stored in the fridge, but don't wash them before you put them in! Berries are very delicate, so keep them dry and covered. Wash them when you're ready to eat them.

- **Other fruits like avocados, apples, bananas, citrus, peaches, and apricots** are best stored out of the fridge. Refrigerating these fruits often results in loss of flavor and an inferior texture.

- **Dairy products, such as milk, cream, butter, yogurt, and cheese,** are best stored on a shelf inside the fridge rather than on the door. The fridge door is its warmest area and is subject to the most temperature fluctuations, so it is not conducive to storing highly perishable foods. Unless you are going through milk and other dairy products very quickly, they would benefit from being on a shelf. Condiments and other well-preserved foods are generally fine on the door.

Execute Your Plan

Once you have a plan sketched out, it is time to bring your vision to life. Below are some helpful tips to consider.

Measure before you buy.
Once you have a good idea of where you believe items would best be stored, measure your drawers and shelves and then go shopping for organizing supplies.

Buy more than you need.
My favorite refrigerator containers are a mix of long clear plastic bins that maximize the depth of the fridge along with food-specific containers like egg bins and soda can holders. The reason I like clear plastic bins inside the refrigerator is they allow you to see what you have and are easy to pull out and clean. Buying more than you need gives you freedom to play around with the design until it works for you. Unused containers can be returned.

Label.
Just like any other space, labeling is important to help people easily find what they are looking for in the refrigerator. Go with broad category labels like dairy rather than milk to provide flexibility.

Organizing a Pantry

A well-organized pantry can save you both time and money. And, when arranged with an eye for design, it can be a place that actually brings you joy. My overarching principle for organizing food and ingredients in the kitchen is to aim for the golden rule of organizing—assign a home for everything. When you follow that principle, you won't buy multiple bottles of something just because you couldn't find the one you already had.

Group, Ditch, Convert, and Label

Group like items together.

I shared this principle earlier in the chapter, but it is especially important to follow in the pantry. Place snacks with snacks, pasta with pasta, oils with oils, and so on. Storing like items together makes it easy to find things quickly. Store smaller items, such as individual granola bars or tubs of applesauce, in bins so they stay together.

Left: Organizing a pantry is half art and half science. Using a mix of materials for the bins to create zones adds visual interest and beauty. **Above left:** *Packaging takes up a lot of space.* **Above right:** *When you take individually packaged items out of their boxes, you are able to fit more into your pantry.*

Ditch the packaging.

Boxes and bags take up space, so for efficiency, remove unnecessary packaging and place products in your new clear containers before putting them away in your pantry or fridge. This also simplifies cooking and baking.

Convert to clear.

I recommend keeping dry items like flour, sugar, rice, and coffee in clear, air-tight containers. Not only will your ingredients stay fresher longer, using clear containers will also allow a quick scan to see when stock is low. When you convert to clear, there is no more overbuying—you'll know exactly when it's time for more lentils.

If you can, I recommend investing in good quality containers that use high density plastic or glass and have seals to keep your foods fresh. While it may not be fun up front to spend the money on this sort of thing, if you choose high-quality, it should be a one-time purchase.

Label everything.

Labeling in a shared space like the pantry—where the whole household is looking for and using items—is nonnegotiable. Keep categories broad so you can buy something different and not need to switch labels. There are so many label options available, from chalk pens to handwriting on or printing out adhesive labels to custom vinyl labels. Choose labels that match your personal style and bring you joy.

Create a Defined Zone for Backstock

I like to create a defined space for backstock, whether it is in the pantry or food cupboard or somewhere more remote. This separates ingredients you use on a daily basis from backup items that you can use when you run out.

If you're tight on space or buy in bulk, a remote backstock location can be a good idea. It could be as simple as a set of shelves in the basement. I recommend shopping your own backstock before going grocery shopping so you don't overbuy.

• *When you have a large pantry, divide it into smaller zones so you can find what you're looking for quickly.*

How to Organize a Clothing Closet

I'm often called in to help someone organize their clothing closet with complaints like "I can't find anything that I'm looking for" and "I've organized, but it gets messy so quickly!" I empathize with their pleas for a better system because I know first-hand that having a closet that isn't working is terrible.

In contrast, when your closet is decluttered and organized, it is so much easier to get ready to leave the house—and much more enjoyable too. It is easier because you will be able to find everything quickly. This means you will be able to find your favorite pair of jeans, your go-to sweater, or your most cherished pair of shoes in the blink of an eye. Doesn't that sound amazing?

Getting dressed is something you do to start your day, so making that process easier helps you get every day started on a positive note. We've all had those mornings where we can't seem to find a clothing item, which causes frustration and can lead to a downward spiral of negative emotions.

Getting your closet in tip-top shape takes a little time and patience, but the rewards of a smooth morning are worth it. In this section, you'll find my best tips for getting your closet into shape. And remember, these tips assume you've already decluttered your entire wardrobe.

Evaluate the System

The first step when organizing a clothing closet or storage system is to evaluate the current system. Look at the three main areas: hanging rods, shelving, and drawers. Determine if they might need an upgrade.

You might ask yourself the following questions.

Hanging rods

Is your hanging rod(s) wood or metal? Is the rod a solid smooth bar where hangers can move easily, or is the rod divided into sections? Is the rod in good condition, or does it need repair? Is it adjustable or fixed? Do you have space to hang both short items like shirts as well as long items like dresses?

Smartly planned zones in a closet can save you time when getting ready in the morning.

Ideally, you will have solid and adjustable hanging rods in your closet that have no dividing sections. Adjustable-height rods allow you to change your closet configuration. For example, if you wear mostly dresses or long sweaters, but your current closet doesn't have room for long items, an upgrade would be ideal. On the other hand, if you have mainly dress shirts and sports coats, a double hung rod might be best.

Shelving

Do you have shelving in or near your closet? Is it solid or wire? If it is wire, are the wires close together or far apart? Is the shelving adjustable or fixed? How many shelves do you currently have?

With solid shelves, you can store high-heeled shoes without the heels falling through, and you can put sweaters on them without the risk of wire marks. But wire shelving can be better in humid climates where you need air flow to prevent mustiness.

Drawers

Do you have any drawers in your current clothes storage system? Do they pull in and out easily? Are they made of plastic, metal, or wood? Quality drawers made of metal or wood should be sturdy, and the drawers should pull out and slide in very smoothly. High-quality drawers might be expensive, but they are likely to last longer.

In my experience, it is most often the closet system itself that has a large part to play in the clutter in the closet, especially with small closets. Unless you have a very minimal wardrobe, builder-grade wire shelves with a hanging rod system or a reach-in closet with one wooden hanging rod below one wooden shelf are not sufficient to successfully organize your clothes.

Sometimes just adding a few extra shelves to your exisiting closet system is enough, while other times, replacing the old system with a completely new one is best. There are many closet organization systems on the market where you can add a couple of screws to hold up the vertical supports and then simply click in shelves or hanging bars.

Now don't get me wrong: I'm not suggesting that you need an entire room for your clothes or that you require an expensive custom closet in order to successfully organize them. What I am suggesting is that you consider buying the best closet system your budget allows. Investing in a closet system—especially in a small closet—maximizes every inch of space and will be some of the best money you will spend on organization.

● *Use every inch of space, including the back of the door, when organizing small closets.*

Organize by Category, then Color

There is no right or wrong way to organize your clothes in a closet, but I like to recommend going first by category, then by color. The reason I like to organize like this is a practical one—it simply makes pulling an outfit together easier.

To organize by category, gather up all of the items from one large subcategory, like shirts, and then divide them into smaller subcategories such as long sleeves, short sleeves, and sleeveless. Then, divide each subcategory into a smaller subcategory. For example, divide long sleeves into collared shirts, long-sleeved blouses, and long-sleeved T-shirts. Do the same for short-sleeved shirts, and so on. Continue to divide all of the large categories.

The reason I like to organize by color within each subcategory is because it makes it very easy for you to see where the new category starts. I also like the streamlined visual organizing. The guide I use for organizing by color is the rainbow (with the addition of white, gray, brown, and black), but use whatever color system works for you. If you want to try the rainbow method, then the order would be white, red, orange, yellow, green, blue, indigo, violet, brown, grey, and black.

File Fold

Some clothing items are best hung on hangers, while other items are better kept folded. In my opinion, scarves, sweaters, T-shirts, and undergarments are best folded. I also believe folded clothes are best inside of drawers rather than on shelves because when you try to get an item of clothing from the middle of a pile of clothes that are stacked on a shelf, you usually mess up the entire shelf of items. When you fold clothes using a method called file folding, you are able to get the garment out of a drawer without making a mess of all of the other items of clothing around it.

The file folding method goes by different names, but the principles remain mostly the same. Fold your garment into a rectangle shape, and then fold it into smaller sections until it stands on its own. This means you can "file" it into the drawer. Filing your clothes when you put them into the drawer makes it easy to see everything all at once.

- *When you file fold your clothes, you are both able to see your options more easily and can pull a clothing item from the drawer without unfolding or messing up the others.*

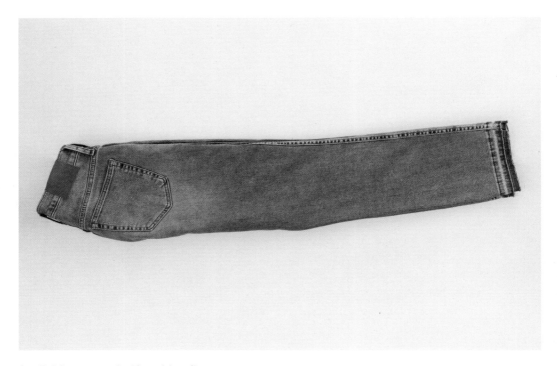

- *Fold pants in half and lay flat.*

- *Tuck in the crotch of the pants and then fold in half from the ankle to the waist, leaving a slight gap.*

- *Fold the pants into thirds.*

- *Continue folding pants into thirds.*

● *When you finish the folding, your clothes should stand nicely on their own.*

- *Lay your shirt face down.*

- *Fold in the sides of your shirt equally and smooth down.*

- *Fold from the bottom of the shirt to the neck of the shirt, leaving a slight gap.*

- *Starting from the neck, fold down in halves or thirds, depending on the size of the shirt.*

● *When you finish the folding, your clothes should stand nicely on their own.*

Switch Things Out Seasonally, if Necessary

If you live in a climate that doesn't change much throughout the year or if layering your clothes is your go-to choice when dressing, then a seasonal switch out might not be worth the effort. Having said that, if the size of your closet is very small or the size of your wardrobe is very large, you might be a good candidate for a seasonal switch out.

Storing more than one season of clothing in a small closet can make it difficult to see and use what you have. But even if you have a really large closet, it can make sense to do a seasonal switch out to streamline how quickly you are able to get ready in the morning and cut down on the choices.

The items to consider switching out are items that are dedicated to one season, which means putting away snow boots and heavy sweaters in the spring and putting away light pants, shorts, and summer dresses in the winter. There are a couple of ways that you can store your seasonal items for maximum care.

The first option is to simply put all of your seasonal items into a spare closet. Move your winter clothes into the spare closet in the summer and vice versa in the winter. The second option is to put your clothes into bins—they could be in plastic totes, covered fabric bins, or open-top fabric bins. Whichever way you choose to store them, make sure the clothes have some space to breathe. Additionally, you can throw a few cedar balls into the bins to keep the pests away during storage.

Match Your Hangers!

If there is one thing you can do today to improve the look of your closet almost instantly, it is to match your hangers. The uniformity removes excess visual clutter, which makes your closet more pleasing to the eye. Another benefit of using matching hangers is that all of your clothes and coats hang at the same height.

How to Organize Laundry (and the Laundry Room)

For some, "laundry" is a four-letter word. For a rare few, it's a treat. Wherever you fall on the spectrum, laundry can be a nuisance if you lack a system to take care of it. Getting a system to organize clothes from start to finish is essential for laundry success, and having a system will help you keep your clothes looking nicer for longer.

Laundry Starts Where You Take Your Clothes Off

Determining where you will put dirty clothes is the first thing you need to consider when organizing laundry. This might be in hampers in each of the bedroom closets or in a small pile of dirty clothes in the corner of the room that you take to the laundry room daily. Whichever way you choose to manage the dirty clothes, the ultimate goal is to get dirty laundry to the laundry room (or to sorting bins if you do laundry remotely) quickly.

Design the Laundry Room or System

A well-designed laundry room or laundry system is a game changer. Designing a way to manage laundry is key because dirty clothes are coming in daily. Without a system, it can all pile up, and the chore of doing the laundry can seem insurmountable. Whether you have a large laundry room or a small space, the organizing considerations shown below can help when designing an organizational system in the laundry area.

- sorting bins
- easy storage for and quick access to laundry supplies
- a place to hang clothes

Having laundry supplies divided into subcategories in an easy-to-reach cabinet helps simplify the laundry routine.

Design with attention and care, and you'll reap the positive benefits of having a beautiful space to do some of the dirtiest and most boring work. Making it user-friendly means everyone can and will use it.

To Sort or Not to Sort

There is a lot of debate about whether it is necessary to sort clothes into whites, darks, and delicates. Some believe sorting is essential for giving clothes the best care, while others believe throwing everything in mixed up saves time and stress. I think it's a matter of personal preference.

Personally, I like to sort by type of clothing, but you could also choose to sort by member of the family. You can ruin clothes by not caring for them properly. I still remember putting something dark in with something white and discoloring the white garment for good! Sorting also makes it easier when you're teaching children to help do laundry. To whatever degree you sort clothes, your organizational system should make that easy and intuitive.

The organizational system could range anywhere from a luxury laundry sorting system on wheels to plastic laundry baskets to simply having piles of different types of clothing on the floor. Whichever option you choose, make sure the system is labeled so it's clear to everyone what items goes where.

Organize Supplies within Reach

Having your most-used laundry supplies within reach of the washer and dryer makes the act of doing laundry much easier. Create subcategories of your laundry cleaning product so you have all of your spot-cleaning items like a toothbrush, spot remover, and a stain bar together. Keep detergents together and dryer items together, and so on. If you do your laundry remotely, have your supplies in a basket or other easy-to-transport bin.

I like to use storage containers to help keep the different categories easier to maintain, but it's not essential. It's also a good idea to place the items you use most so that they are in the easiest place to reach and arrange any specialty items like dry cleaning products, washing machine cleaning products, and lingerie bags in an out-of-the-way location since you will not reach for them as often.

Shared Laundry/Laundromat

For those of you who don't have laundry in your living space, there are a few special considerations to think about to keep yourself organized on wash day when you need to take laundry on the go.

- **Sorting bins** with handles are easy to transport. Also, consider collapsible sorting bins so they can be transported back home on wash day when they are empty.
- **Laundry supplies** can be kept in a plastic tote with a handle so you can carry all of your wash day essentials together.
- **Collapsible laundry baskets** make it easy for you to transport your bags to the space where you do laundry and also provide you with loads of space after you've folded your clothes from the dryer.
- **Hangers** are still essential. Even if a hanging rod is not an option, you can still hang your clothes. Simply bring hangers with you and hang them up. When you have a full basket of folded laundry, lay the hanging clothes nicely on top and transport them home.

Hanging Space

Having space to hang clothes either to air dry or to finish drying is helpful for keeping your clothes looking their best for a long time. If you have the space to design a hanging rod for your laundry room, you will be pleased with that addition. If you don't, buying a simple portable hanging rod and/ or drying rack can be a great option and can be a space saver as well.

- Glass jars can beautifully showcase bathroom essentials.

- When space is tight, consider using the back of the toilet as a place to store some items.

How to Organize a Bathroom

I've always had small bathrooms in all the homes I've lived in. Maybe that's why I'm so passionate about organizing them. When you have a small bathroom, you quickly realize the importance of only having what you need in the space and nothing more.

When I started organizing homes with larger bathrooms, I realized that using the small-space strategies work very well in larger bathrooms too. You can focus on using the bathroom as you need it, rather than using it as a place to manage storage of bathroom items. Too often when we have extra space available, we fill it in a way that makes it more difficult to maintain.

Keep Active Items and Backstock Items Separate

One rule critical to keeping a bathroom organized is to keep active items and backstock items separate. Only put items you are actively using in the shower, and put any backstock items in a bathroom cabinet or a linen closet. Do not add any items into the shower until you've used up the bottle or product you are using or have chosen to discard it when decluttering. Way too often, I find that my clients have too many bottles of half-used shampoo/conditioner and several choices of body soap. When I ask if they are all being used, the answer is usually no.

Same goes for any cabinets inside the bathroom. Put the items you are actively using in containers you can easily grab and use on a daily basis, and put the backstock of those items in a different place. Keeping them together leads you to open a new bottle of moisturizer before realizing you already had one opened, and soon you have three or four bottles open as well as a cluttered bathroom.

Medicine Cabinet Considerations

Medicine cabinets can be a wonderful storage solution, especially for bathrooms without under-the-sink cabinets. When organizing a medicine cabinet, follow the same rules as any other space by determining your zones and using containers to help you divide the products inside the cabinet. However, since the space is usually limited, consider only organizing your MVPs (most valuable products) into the medicine cabinet. Less is more for medicine cabinet organization.

If you have kids, consider using plastic divided pencil cups to hold tooth-brushes and toothpaste so they can easily come out of the medicine cabinet for use and then be placed right back in when finished. Keeping items off the counters in the bathroom helps with ongoing cleaning.

Storing Medicine

I find a lot of medicine in bathrooms, but the heat and moisture from your shower, bath, and sink can damage or decrease the shelf life of some medications. It's best to store medicine in a cool, dry space.

● *Use containers to divide the products in your medicine cabinet to help keep the small space tidy.*

Organizing Under the Sink

Many people have under-the-sink cabinets, which can be tricky to organize since the pipes of the sink get in the way.

If your under-the-sink cabinet doesn't have any drawers, adding containers with drawers is a great option. Having drawers under the sink allows you to pull contents like toothpaste and face wash quickly out of a drawer and then easily put them back.

If you are lucky enough to have drawers in the cabinet in your bathroom, find drawer organizers to divide the drawer and create homes for the sub-categories you use most often.

Choosing Bins and Storage

When choosing bins and storage for the bathroom, you should keep a couple of things in mind. The first is the type of product that is going to be stored in the bin. If the product might leak, then it's a good idea to have a container that you can easily clean, which makes plastic and bamboo good choices.

The second thing to keep in mind is the humidity in the bathroom. Some storage products, and some beauty products for that matter, are best stored in a dry place and are best kept out of the bathroom. Uncoated fiberboard boxes don't usually mix well with moisture, so those are best to keep outside of a bathroom environment. Stick with plastic and wire in the bathroom. Glass is okay as long as it isn't in a place where small children could knock it over.

- *Under-the-sink storage can be a nice place in which to keep extra towels or toilet paper.*

How to Organize Toys

Toys are a sensitive topic because all too often organizing the toys really isn't the real problem. I know this because I, too, once thought my overflowing toy box was an organizing problem. After years of my own challenges organizing and managing my children's toys, I realized the actual challenge in keeping toys organized is setting and managing volume.

Often, kids have too many toys, and that's why parents and children struggle to keep the toys organized. Parents (and grandparents) usually have the best intentions, but buying too much of a good thing can lead to a lot of challenges.

And while bins and boxes will help to organize the toys and help children to manage them better, the larger issues of volume and management need to be addressed. To that end, let's address organizing toys from all angles, including how to organize the bins and boxes.

Determine the Right Number of Toys Before You Buy

When it comes to toys, it's really important for parents to consider, discuss, and agree on how many toys they believe is the right number. Determining what you, as parents, believe is the Goldilocks amount before your child has something to say about it is key.

In a study conducted at the University of Toledo, researchers found that an environment with fewer toys is better for kids. The research studied a group of toddlers and gave them either four or sixteen toys. The study revealed that kids who were given fewer toys focused more, were more engaged, played more creatively, and interacted with their toys in more varied ways for longer periods of time. The study concluded that there was a significant difference in the quality of toddlers' play between the two conditions.

● *Using baskets and bins to divide subcategories of toys helps children know where to put the toys when they are done playing.*

Create a Decluttering Routine

Managing the incoming volume of toys is an ongoing challenge every parent needs to address. Children outgrow toys, and trying to discard toddler toys when your children are ten is harder than getting rid of them as you go.

You will be able to keep a very good handle on your toys if you declutter your kids' toys seasonally, which is about every three months. This is a rough guideline rather than a rule. Some families might find a more frequent decluttering routine would be best, while other families might find that a less frequent routine might be the ticket. Whichever frequency you choose, twice per year is the minimum.

Getting in the habit of routinely taking stock of children's toys is the best way to be successful in keeping the toys organized.

It is important to involve your children in the decluttering process. Children are keenly aware of what toys they love and what toys no longer bring them joy. Getting kids to learn early on that items have a life cycle and it's okay to say goodbye to something when its life cycle is complete is an important lesson.

Please don't throw away or donate your children's toys without their permission. Doing this leads to a loss of trust. Additionally, when you make the decisions for your children, they will not acquire the ability to say goodbye and move on, which could be a challenge as an adult.

One In, One Out Rule

For some people, a rule is helpful when determining how to manage a category of items where the volume is constantly changing. Toys is one of those categories. A rule that can be helpful when managing toys is a "one in, one out" rule.

It is a simple concept and literally means that when your child gets a new toy, they need to say goodbye to one. If you have organized your child's toys to a manageable level, the one in, one out rule will help you keep on top of the volume. This strategy would become your decluttering routine.

Address the Guilt

One thing I bump into over and over when helping parents declutter their children's toys is guilt. And let me be clear about whose guilt we're talking about here—it's the parent's guilt, not the children's guilt.

Since children tend to get a lot of toys as gifts, guilt can show up when decluttering children's toys. I'm not immune to this either. My son got a beautiful barn built by his grandfather. He loved the barn and played with it a lot—until he didn't. And then the barn just took up a lot of space in our basement. When I asked my son if he loved it and used it anymore, he said no. He said we could donate it to someone else who could love it.

I kept that barn around for almost a year after that conversation and finally decided it was time for it to go. We didn't have the space; my child didn't want it and Grandpa would love us regardless. I took it to a donation site, and the person taking the donation was enthusiastic, saying that he already knew of a different child would simply love it. I felt good knowing it was going to a great home.

Addressing keeping things out of guilt is always important. As parents, if you haven't addressed your own guilt with gifts, you can pass it on to your children.

Build trust with your *children* by having them choose what stays and what goes.

Create a Space to Play

When determining where to organize your toys, the first step is to determine how much space your kids need to play. If you use all of the space you have to organize the toys and do not leave any space for the kids to actually play with the toys, you've defeated the purpose of toys.

To that end, the first step in organizing toys is to determine how much play space you want to have, whether it is open floor space, wall space, and/or flat surface space. Once you have that vision in mind, it's time to start organizing the toys.

Organize by Category and Ditch the Lids

Just like with clothes, I like to organize toys into subcategories. I like to put board games with board games, cars with cars, blocks with blocks, and so on. There is no exact rule for how many categories to create since it depends on the volume and size of the items you have. For example, if your child has three different sets of trains and likes to play with them individually, you might opt to categorize them by type of train. On the other hand, if your child likes to used the three different sets together, you could categorize them under one large category.

While there are times when you should use lids in a play space, a general rule of thumb to organizing a place where children will be responsible for cleaning up is to ditch the lids. Selecting bins and baskets without lids makes cleanup easier, and the easier you can make cleanup, the better chance that your children will do it.

How to Organize Your Home Checklist

☐ **Assign a home for everything.** This is the most important step in organizing a home. Without assigning a home for everything you own, you leave a lot of ambiguity about where things should go when they need to be put away.

☐ **Divide larger spaces into zones.** When you divide larger spaces, such as kitchens, into zones, you are able to focus on smaller challenge areas at one time.

☐ **Store like with like.** Putting similar items in one place in the home makes it easy for you to know the volumes of those items and find what you're looking for when you need it.

☐ **Subcategorize into managable categories.** Dividing similar items into smaller, more manageable categories makes it much more likely you will be able to maintain the organizational system you've created.

☐ **Label.** Labels are the road signs for the items that live in your home. They provide everyone using the home with clear directions on where items live and where they need to go when it's time to put them back. Even if you live alone, labels take the memory guesswork out of where something goes.

HOW TO KEEP YOUR HOME ORGANIZED

5

There isn't a magic potion or a magic wand. The power to keep your home organized lies within you.

If you've decluttered and organized your home successfully in the past but have had a difficult time keeping it that way, you're not alone. Let's look at some of the reasons why you may be having difficulties keeping your home organized along with practical recommendations for what you can do about it. We will examine more deeply how time clutter and mental clutter might be the reasons it's been difficult for you to maintain a tidy and organized home.

I believe everyone can have a tidy and organized home. Yes, I mean everyone! I'm bold in my belief because I have witnessed miraculous decluttering and organizing transformations over the years. I've walked into homes where I couldn't see one clear surface transformed into a space where all surfaces were free of clutter and everything had a home. Even more convincing is that I've visited these homes many months later to find them almost exactly as I had left it.

Of course, I have also witnessed equally amazing transformations that haven't seemed to stick in the same way. As I learned more and helped more people declutter and organize, I began to see some patterns emerge with the ones that stuck and the ones that had more trouble. Equally, I began to see further transformations once clients and I were able to discuss some of the underlying challenges of time and mental clutter and how they played a role.

The reality is that keeping your home organized is simple. You put your things back to their homes when you're done using them. However, it requires a commitment of time and energy as well as participation from everyone in the home.

In order for you to see a lasting change, you must dig in a bit and get curious about why you have struggled to keep your spaces clutter free in the past. Once you understand why you struggle, you will be better able to confront your struggle and achieve lasting change.

- *When you have a home for items you use daily, such as a dog leash or a light jacket, you can perform your daily tasks with ease.*

Why It Hasn't Worked in the Past

There are many possible reasons why you have not been able to keep your home clutter free and tidy despite your best intentions. What's important is figuring out where you've gotten stuck in the past so you can take steps to move forward differently this time around. What follows are the most common challenges I've observed for people who've tried to declutter and organize, but seemed to have trouble making it stick.

You Didn't Finish Your Decluttering Marathon

Have you ever become so tired of the clutter in your house that you charged into decluttering with gusto but then lost steam and didn't finish the whole house? Maybe you were able to declutter a few categories of items like clothes and books or one room but then stopped. If you've experienced this, you're not alone.

It isn't uncommon to start a whole-house decluttering effort and lose momentum before you finish. But, if you've never finished decluttering your entire home, it is likely you didn't create homes for everything you own either. And, as you know from reading this far in the book, having a home for everything you own is essential to how you create (and then maintain) an organized home.

So, if you're struggling keeping your home organized and clutter free, maybe the reason is that you haven't actually finished the first step properly, and you need to take a few steps back before you can move forward.

Having a clutter-free home is possible for everyone, but it does require some commitment.

CLIENT CHRONICAL: DECLUTTERING, BUT LEFT WITH TOO MUCH

Sometimes, even after you've decluttered, the volume of items you own is too much. I had a client, we'll call her Janet, who had enough greeting cards and stationery that she could have written a card or thank you note every day for five years without buying anything new. On the first pass of reviewing her stationery, Janet kept almost everything.

A few months later, when decluttering a new space in her home, we found more cards and stationery that she had forgotten about. I urged Janet to review the whole category again since it's essential to review a full category at one time to decide what to keep. She agreed.

This time, we dug deeper into why she loved certain cards and how she was going to use them. We then did some math to figure out how long this number of cards would last. By going through them one at a time, she realized that there were actually some cards she didn't like anymore and that the volume was not manageable. In the end, she donated approximately 30 to 40 percent of the collection. She was left with an amount that was manageable and only contained her favorites.

As for what is the just right amount, only you will know. The rule is simple—it's the amount you can manage. If you find yourself having a difficult time managing all of the items in your home, you likely would benefit from having fewer items.

You're Not Allocating Enough Time for Daily Tasks

One of the most common complaints I hear from people when I ask why it is difficult for them to keep their homes clutter free and organized is that they don't feel they have enough time.

You might find that you underestimate how long it takes to fully complete a task. For example, you might estimate it takes thirty minutes to get ready in the morning but then realize at the thirty-minute mark that you don't have enough time to put away the hair, face, and body products you used to get yourself ready or to properly sort your dirty laundry. So instead of putting those items away, you leave them where they are and rush out the door to make it to wherever you need to be. This cycle is common and always leads to a trail of clutter.

Given that time is one of the major challenges with keeping a home, and your mind for that matter, clutter free, we've dedicated an entire chapter in this book to decluttering your time (see page 139). Until you learn to organize your time, you'll struggle to organize many areas of your life.

You're Letting Your Mood Run the Show

Sometimes, you just might not feel like putting your stuff away. You might be too tired, too grumpy, or too something else and just don't want to do it. When I've asked some people why their houses seem to get cluttered, they've told me that they just don't feel in the mood to put their stuff away after a long day.

Let's consider what happens when you let your mood run the show. When you put a brush down on the counter rather than in its home or leave mail on the counter for days rather than sorting it quickly and recycling it, you are adding items to your to-do list. What happens is that instead of spending five to ten minutes a day putting things back, you end up with little bits of clutter all over the house, and you then need to find an hour (or so it seems) to put your things away.

Now, if you live alone, you might think it doesn't matter whether you put your stuff away because you are responsible for everything. But here's the thing, because putting things away and keeping your home organized falls 100 percent on you, inattention can overwhelm and lead to negative self-talk and feelings of anxiety. I've seen this time and time again with my single clients. My clients who live alone know that decluttering and organizing efforts all fall on them, so it requires internal motivation rather than external motivation. This is why it's especially important to be mindful throughout the day and put things away as you finish using them. Doing little bits all day long is much more manageable than letting it go for weeks and then resenting your past decisions and feeling too overwhelmed to lift a finger.

For those who have children, letting your mood run the show also has repercussions. It won't be easy to hold your children accountable to put their things away when they are done using them if you don't put your own things away. Children learn most from "do as I do" lessons rather than "do as I say."

You've Convinced Yourself That You're "Messy"

I don't believe people are inherently messy or tidy. I believe everyone is a little bit of both. Labeling yourself as messy is self-defeating. Instead, think of how you can reframe yourself. If you would like to live more intentionally and not be surrounded by clutter, you need to make the conscious decision that you can.

● *Keeping spaces where you do a lot of daily tasks, such as a laundry room, clutter free can improve your spirit when you're doing the work.*

The Art of Keeping a Tidy Home

The art of keeping your home tidy, even if you have children, is something you can achieve with a little bit of focus and follow-through.

Don't Put It Down, Put It Away

The closest thing to giving you a magic wand to keep your home tidy is to have you follow one simple guideline. Put your things back to their "home" when you are done using them. While it will not always be easy for you to follow the guideline, it truly is the secret to keeping a home tidy once and for all.

A special note for parents: As is true with so many aspects of parenting, it's important for you to lead by example when it comes to putting your stuff away. It's difficult for kids to understand why they should put their things away when you are not putting your things away. You have to work on developing yourself in this area as you begin to hold your kids accountable to do the same.

For the next 24 hours, I challenge you to be very mindful about exactly what you do with your things when you are done using them. Where do you put your toothbrush when you're done with it? When you come in the door of your house, what do you do with your bag, wallet, or keys? What about your coat? Where do you put the mail when you get it from the mailbox? Be mindful and watch your behavior closely to see if you can find a pattern in how you put or don't put things away in their home.

Once you've observed yourself for 24 hours, spend the next 24 hours being very mindful and present about putting everything back in its home when you're done using it. Try your very best to stay with each task until it is complete. Reflect on how easy or difficult it was for you to stay in the moment, and reflect on what went well and what got in your way.

- *When you have a place for everything in your home and you keep everything in its place, your home will be (and stay) tidy.*

Hold Your Kids Accountable (and Your Spouse/ Partner/Roommate Too)

Do you feel like you are always picking up socks, shoes, and other items left around the house every day by your kids and/or your partner? Do you get frustrated having to ask your kids and/or your partner over and over to put their things away? Do you often choose to put everything away yourself because you think it's just easier and faster if you do it yourself? If so, you're not alone.

In the short run, it might be easier do everything yourself. It goes faster, it is done the way you want it done, and there doesn't need to be an argument with anyone about anything. On some level, it feels like a more peaceful path. Unfortunately, this might not be the most peaceful path in the long run.

The best advice I learned as an adult was to start as you mean to go on. This advice is simple and can be applied to so many areas of our lives. It requires you to think about what kind of home environment you want to create.

For example, if you want to create a home environment where everyone in the family actively participates, then it is important to establish a set of agreed-upon rules when the relationship is young. If you don't want to pick up after your partner when they are fifty, then don't pick up after them the week after the honeymoon. If you don't want to pick up your children's rooms when they are in high school, then don't pick up their rooms when they are three, four, and five.

Another important part of "starting as you mean to go on" is that it requires open and honest conversation. If you hope that your partner, spouse, or children will just know what your heart desires, you will be disappointed. They will not. Instead, you need to tell them and find out how to work together to make it a success.

Once you've established the rules or boundaries in the relationship, it is time to hold the people in the relationship accountable for their end of the bargain. Holding kids accountable helps them grow into mature and responsible adults. Holding partners and spouses accountable lessens the amount of resentment you might feel.

Don't lose hope if you're in a five-, ten-, twenty-, or thirty-year relationship already because you can start at any point. Just like so many decisions in a long-term relationship, it's important to have a conversation and get on the same page when you feel something isn't quite where you want it to be. If you're feeling like clutter is getting in the way of your relationship or your ideal life together, take the time to talk about it as a couple and begin with envisioning what your ideal future state looks like. (You can do this with roommates too!) Rehashing how you got here will not provide a lot of benefit, so take your time to share your concerns with your partner, and create a vision for the future. Use the conversation as your springboard for starting as you mean to go on together.

Get Help if You Need It

Sometimes, you need a little help to get you from point A to point B on a home project, and decluttering and organizing your home is no exception. Just as you might hire a gardening service to weed your garden or a plumber to clean out your pipes or a cleaning person to clean your home, you might need to hire a professional organizer to help you declutter and organize your home, giving you a head start and a strong foundation for keeping it organized.

Don't feel defeated if organizing isn't your strength. If it's not, then maybe it's time to partner with someone whose strength it is.

A Special Note for People with Chronic Disorganization

Chronic disorganization is having a past history of disorganization in which all self-help efforts to change have failed. The reasons for chronic disorganization are varied and might include physical or mental illness, ADHD, or hoarding tendencies. If you believe you have chronic disorganization, some of the solutions in this book might help you, but you also might need to seek out specific help from a professional who specializes in chronic disorganization as they might have different solutions to help your specific challenges.

Establishing Home Organization Routines

Adults, much like children, function better when their lives are centered around routines. When you set routines, you are able to complete repetitive activities without exerting as much mental energy because completing tasks in the same order repeatedly builds brain power and mental muscle, allowing your brain to work less for the same result. And who doesn't want that?

Routines can also help you feel comfortable in a fast-paced, complex world. Having a familiar flow to your day can save you time, can make you more efficient, and can help get you firing on all cylinders. While each day is different because the tasks, action items, and events may vary, having a routine provides a solid framework and a sensible sequence.

Most importantly, routines help you keep your home organized.

Having kids routinely put their toys away beginning at a small age will help build life skills they can draw upon in the future.

The Morning Routine

How you begin your day, whether rested and focused or frazzled, typically sets the tone for the rest of it. Your morning routine should be your daily constant. Mornings need not be rushed or chaotic if you have a routine you follow that covers all the necessary things (including a realistic amount of time!) to get you out the door. There is no such thing as one perfect morning routine. A perfect morning routine is one that is perfect for you, but there are some tips that can help you.

If you find yourself (or your family) rushing in the morning, it's time to consider getting up earlier. Getting up just fifteen minutes earlier each day can be what you need to enjoy your morning coffee or tea a little longer, prepare your mind for the day ahead, help orchestrate your children's morning, and give you extra time to put away toiletry products and breakfast dishes.

You might also consider exercising in the morning as it boosts your metabolism for the rest of the day. This could be a walk/jog, a trip to the gym, yoga, or even dancing around with your kids or by yourself! You do not have to work out hard. A simple morning stretch routine is enough to get your blood pumping.

Finally, limiting distractions in the morning can help you stay focused, so you might consider staying unplugged for the first hour after you wake up. Checking social media and your inbox can start your day off on the wrong foot. Your morning will be far easier to manage if you aren't distracted at the crack of dawn by the unexpected news and tasks that might be waiting for you in your texts or emails.

● *Establishing and following a morning routine can help get your days started on the right foot.*

The Weekly Reset

A weekly reset is taking time one day each week to reset your home and prepare for the week ahead. When done routinely, a weekly reset helps prepare your mind for the week ahead—starting with a clutter-free tidy home. The main categories touched upon each week during the weekly reset include calendar, meal planning/prep, cleaning, and care.

Calendar

The two main ways to keep a calendar are paper and electronic. Spending focused time each week to review your calendar helps you see the full picture of activities for you and your family and helps your brain start to prepare for the week ahead. (For more, see chapter 6.)

Meal planning/prep

Mealtime can feel overwhelming, but with a little planning ahead, it doesn't need to be. Setting aside 15 minutes to look at your weekly activities and to chose a meal for each night that makes sense based on your schedule are all you need to do to make a meal plan. A rule of thumb is to consider faster meals for busier nights and make more complicated meals when you can set aside the time to do so.

Once you have your meal plan set, take time to prep food for the week. Cutting up or roasting vegetables and cooking grains in bulk can be huge timesavers for busy weekday evenings. If you have children, having them help you prep lunch and snack items for the week can also save you oodles of time and teach them an important life skill.

Cleaning

The two areas of focus in cleaning for the weekly reset are putting everything back into its proper home and cleaning areas that need attention. If you're doing a great job of putting your stuff away when you're done using it, this might only take a few minutes each week. Then you can give some extra attention to cleaning areas that need your attention like taking out the garbage and cleaning bathrooms, kitchen sinks, and counters.

Care

Giving care to items that need it, including ourselves, is an important part of the weekly reset. This might consist of watering indoor plants, hand-washing clothing that needs extra care, or simply taking a long bath and relaxing. I recommend doing the care part as the last step in the weekly reset as a treat.

● *Meal prep is a fun and effective way to bring organization into the kitchen.*

Decluttering Routine

It would be easy to think that once you've decluttered your entire home, you are done decluttering forever, but that's not true. It's important to establish ongoing decluttering routines because new items will come into your possession after you've finished your decluttering marathon.

A decluttering routine is simply doing regular checks on your things to ensure they still bring you joy and to discard the ones that do not. The categories most suited for a decluttering routine are clothes/shoes, books, seasonal items, and papers.

Clothes/shoes
Bringing new things into the closet is the time to review and consider if everything still warrants a spot, so decluttering seasonally is a good rule of thumb.

Books
The number of times you should declutter books depends on the number of books you buy. If you're buying and reading many new books each month, decluttering seasonally might make a lot of sense. On the other hand, if you're only buying a few books a year, you will not need to declutter as often.

Seasonal items
Items purchased to celebrate seasons can take up a lot of storage space, so it is important to declutter seasonal items every time you take out the bins to put up the seasonal décor.

Papers
Papers can stack up quickly, so it is most ideal to handle paper clutter (e.g., mail) daily, and review papers generally each week. Another great time of year to declutter papers is when you are preparing your taxes.

How to Keep Your Home Organized Checklist

☐ **Dig in deeper to see why keeping your home organized hasn't worked in the past.** This will help you choose solutions that will help you succeed as you move forward.

☐ **Put your things away after you're done using them.** One guideline of keeping a house tidy is to put your things away after you're done using them. If you follow this one rule every time you used something, you will never have a disorganized home.

☐ **Hold your spouse/partner/kids/roommates accountable.** Holding everyone accountable to help keep common spaces tidy and organized is required. Without accountability, one person feels as if they need to do everything, which often leads to resentment.

☐ **Get help if you need it.** If decluttering was easy, but organizing or staying organized is more difficult for you, then it's time to consider hiring someone to help you.

☐ **Establish strong routines.** Once your home is decluttered and organized, strong routines can help you easily keep it that way for life.

DECLUTTERING YOUR DAY

Once you realize that you alone decide how to spend your time, you open up a new world of possibility.

Ask most people how busy they are, and you might hear them say, "I always feel rushed," or, "There's just too much to do," or simply, "I'm overwhelmed," or, "I'm busy!"

While people you and I talk to are likely to tell us they are working more and are busier than ever, research tells us that it's not true. People are actually working less and sleeping more today than compared to fifty years ago, according to several research studies by Johnathan Gershuny at the University College London's Centre for Time Use Research. The researchers used data from British diaries where people kept track of their time dating back as far as 1961 along with other time diaries collected across the globe to showcase the reality of how we use our time.

Let's explore some hypotheses on why it seems everyone feels more time crunched than ever. One hypothesis suggests the cultural shifts in the attitudes toward work and leisure have resulted in busy as a "badge of honor." This type of thinking raises being busy to a status symbol, which encourages you to showcase and communicate to everyone just how busy you are.

Another hypothesis is the sheer number of choices we have in our tech-driven, always connected world contributes to our feeling of too much to do. No longer is keeping up with the Joneses limited to simply wanting what they have, but we also want to do what they do, leaving ourselves overbooked and overcommitted.

I believe many of us are also losing time simply managing all of our stuff. On a global scale, people are buying more than ever, and each item requires time to care for and manage it.

In this chapter, we are going to look at practical ways for you to gain control of how you spend your time. We will dig into practical ways for how you can prioritize effectively, how you can improve decision-making, and how to keep track of it all.

- *Visual clutter, especially in your work environment, can affect your productivity.*

The Power of Prioritization

I'm not the only one who has hit the end of the day without accomplishing what I thought I might. Often, when I look at those days with curiosity, I realize I didn't quite have a clear picture of what my priorities were at the start of the day. Other times, the clutter in my mind was stronger than my focus to move forward on my priorities.

Regardless of why you don't get done what you need to get done, it can be frustrating and can lead to a vicious downward spiral. It's important to recognize when it's time to stop, to redirect yourself toward your priorities, and to get moving in a positive forward direction. Your goal is to get your momentum moving in the direction of your priorities.

Prioritizing is a powerful tool that provides clarity on what actions you need to take. And, conversely, it shows which actions you should stop taking.

Prioritizing is very straightforward in theory. But in practice, it can be difficult because there are so many things competing for your attention: your family, your friends, and the never-ending call of electronics and screens.

Having the opportunity to choose is a wonderful privilege. It is up to you to decide how you choose to spend the 24 hours you are given each day and with whom you will spend them. So, it is you who decides what your priorities are for your day.

Write It Down

The first step to prioritizing what you need to accomplish is to write it all down. When you write things down, you don't have to keep so much information in the forefront of your mind. Additionally, writing your priorities down allows you to see them differently and evaluate them more clearly.

Choosing what you will NOT do during your work day is as important as choosing what you will do. Prioritization is critical to a clutter-free day.

To start, I recommend a good old-fashioned brain dump, which is just getting out a blank piece of paper and writing down what you believe you need to accomplish. Don't judge what you are writing down; just write projects and tasks down until you can't think of anything else.

Please resist the urge to dive right in and start crossing tasks off your brain dump list as it is your starting point, not your ending point. Working straight from a brain dump assumes that everything on the page is equal.

Evaluate

Once you have finished your brain dump, it's time to start evaluating each of the tasks. A tool I've used for many years to evaluate priorities is the urgent vs. important matrix such as the the one at right. (It's often called the Eisenhower matrix, as President Eisenhower used this method to prioritize.) The matrix consists of four quadrants that classify your daily activities according to two parameters: level of urgency and level of importance.

The urgent vs. important matrix can be used to prioritize on a variety of levels from long-range projects and tasks to monthly and weekly projects and tasks.

The matrix also helps you combat the "mere urgency" effect, which is a tendency to pursue urgency over importance. According to research conducted by the *Journal of Consumer Research*, people are more likely to perform unimportant tasks over important tasks when the unimportant tasks are characterized merely by spurious urgency. It is because the draw of urgent needs is so strong that we have to hone our skills at determining what is truly important.

After you have practiced using the urgent vs. important matrix, you might be able to skip the brain dump phase and go straight to filling in the matrix. If you are new to prioritizing or new to the matrix, both steps are important.

Quadrant 1 (Q1): Do

When you're working on projects or tasks in quadrant 1, you often feel like you're operating in emergency mode. The work requires your immediate attention because it's urgent (time sensitive) and because you've deemed it important. Q1 includes items of crisis, pressing problems, and close deadlines.

Some examples:

- finishing a time-sensitive report
- responding to time-sensitive emails
- bringing a sick child to the doctor
- solving a pressing problem for a client
- finding a contractor for a house problem

	Urgent	Not Urgent

IMPORTANT

Q1
Important and Urgent

- Crisis
- Pressing problems
- Close deadlines
- Some calls and emails

Q2
Important and Not Urgent

- Planning and Preparation
- Thinking
- Relationship building
- Planned rest

NOT IMPORTANT

Q3
Not Important and Urgent

- Other people's priorities
- Interruptions
- Some calls and emails

Q4
Not Important and Not Urgent

- Busy work
- Escape activities
- Procrastination activities

Often Q1 items either pop up on us unexpectedly, like a sudden illness, a client calling with an urgent need, a last-minute deadline assigned to you, or car trouble. Or they could be tasks that you've put off until you're faced with a clear deadline. Regardless of how they made their way onto your task list, Q1 tasks are inevitable.

The lure of the urgency is what can make so many people spend so much of their time on non-essential, but urgent activities that can fall into Q1 and Q3.

It's important to be efficient with your time when working on items in Q1 in order to ensure you have enough energy left for the most important quadrant, which is Q2. If you're spending every minute feeling as if you're putting out fires, you will feel more stress and anxiety.

Special note: Be careful to notice if the excess pressure and urgency are being placed on you by your own mind.

Quadrant 2 (Q2): Schedule

When you're working on projects or tasks in quadrant 2, you feel calm and in control because you are putting your mind power toward longer-term goals without the time pressures. Q2 activities bring you closer to your goals but don't have the urgent deadlines like Q1. So Q2 is where you want to be as much of the time as you can. Q2 projects include planning/preparing, professional/personal development, and relationship building.

Some examples:

- strategic planning
- attending a professional development course
- exercising
- researching for a project or a vacation
- thinking about larger challenges

Q2 projects and tasks are easy to put off because they're not urgent. However, kicking Q2 activities down the road usually lands them squarely in Q1, which is not ideal because then you will have the added pressure of a time constraint. Doing this leads to unnecessary stress and usually doesn't yield optimal results.

It's critical to schedule time on your calendar for Q2 activities. Not only is it important to reserve time on your calendar for these activities but it's also important for you to schedule them during the time of day when you are at your best and have the most energy. Know what time you do your best work and plan your Q2 activities accordingly.

Quadrant 3 (Q3): Delegate or delay

In quadrant 3, you often feel like you're working on other people's priorities or emergencies and are not able to spend time on activities related to your top priorities. Like Q1, Q3 projects and tasks have the lure of urgency, but what sets Q3 activities apart is that they are not actually important to you.

Some examples:

- checking email or texts when you hear the notification
- taking action on short-term offers
- interruptions from others
- meetings called by others without a clear purpose

The trickiest thing about the items that fall into Q3 is they often come with pressure from other people, which can create internal struggles. You might feel a sense that you should do it out of rank, loyalty, or even friendship. You can try delegating and automating items that come into this quadrant as much as possible to avoid spending too much time on them, but probably the most useful solution for items that fall into this quandrant is a polite "no."

Quadrant 4 (Q4): Delete

In quadrant 4, you don't feel like you're making progress toward your goals. The time-wasting activities in Q4 are often busywork or escapism activities not related to your goals. It is important to be on the lookout for how much time you're spending on Q4 activities and to do your best to diminish or eliminate them. Doing so will increase your productivity and will allow you to focus on more important tasks.

Some examples:

- watching TV excessively
- shopping or browsing online excessively
- mindless scrolling on social media
- rearranging papers on your desk rather than taking action on them
- organizing emails rather than answering them

Don't get leisure activities confused with Q4 activities since planned leisure that is consistent with your goals is a Q2 activity, not a Q4. Planning and taking a trip is a productive Q2 activity, while endless online browsing to take your mind off working on Q1 and Q2 tasks is an unproductive Q4 activity. Often, when you spend too much time on Q4 activities, you will feel further away from your goals, and that can dampen your mood even more, making it more difficult to find your way out of the Q4 time trap.

Estimate

I was diligent at writing down and crossing items off a to-do list for decades before I was introduced to an important step in the process: time estimating. To be fair, I had been instinctively estimating how long different tasks might take, but I hadn't been deliberate about it.

I, like many of you, learned how poor time estimates can bite you in the end. You may tell your boss you can get a report done in an hour, but it takes you two. You think it will take you only two hours to paint your bathroom, and it takes a day. You get the picture.

Psychologists Daniel Kahneman and Amos Tversky identified this phenomenon in 1977. The planning fallacy, as they called it, describes the tendency to underestimate the amount of time it will take to complete a task. In 2011, Kahneman expanded the original idea in his book called *Thinking Fast and Slow*, suggesting that estimation mistakes can usually be attributed to two key factors: failing to consider how long it's taken to complete similar tasks in the past and assuming we won't run into any complications that will cause delays.

Look at the items on your urgent vs. important matrix or your daily to-do list, and estimate how long each of the tasks will take. By taking the time to estimate how long things will take before you do them, you begin to teach yourself how long things will really take.

When I did this dutifully for two weeks, I learned that I was a downright terrible time estimator. I underestimated how long it would take to complete things I was passionate and excited to work on. Conversely, I overestimated how much time it would take to do items I was less excited about.

The reality is that determining how much you can accomplish in a day is a math exercise. Time estimates give you the data you need in order to determine what you can finish in a day, a month, or a year.

It's critical for us to take heart and think about what it is that we are focusing our efforts on. When we know what life we're trying to create, we can choose wisely when deciding how to divide our time.

Until you learn to *organize your time,* you'll struggle to organize other areas of your life.

Day Planning Estimator Exercise

For a week, go through each item on your daily to-do list and write down beside each task how long you think the task will take to complete. Then, once you've completed a task, take a different color pen or pencil and log how long it actually took you to complete the task. Do this every day for at least a week.

At the end of the week, take some time to look at the time estimates vs. the actual time. Do you see any patterns emerge? Were there consistent times of the day or days of the week where your time estimates were off? Were there any types of tasks that consistently seemed to have less-accurate time estimates? Are there any tasks that you could streamline to make them take less time next time?

Decide

Sometimes we don't believe we have a choice in what we do, but how you spend your time is yours alone to decide. If you're in a job you do not like, you have the choice to leave it. If you are being asked to do things that are outside of your competence or passion, you have the choice to have a conversation with the person who is asking you to do it. If your home is cluttered, you have the choice to declutter it. If you have children who don't help you do things around the house, you have the choice to take the time to teach them and hold them accountable.

The truth that you alone control your time might frustrate you. For me sometimes it's easier to believe that someone else is forcing me to make a choice rather than owning up to it myself. You might be coming up with excuses why things cannot change, but that is a story you are telling yourself in your mind. It is an important mental roadblock to get through.

So, approach each day, week, and month as an opportunity to hone your skills in deciding what steps you will take toward your life's goals and passions. Every 24 hours is a new chance for you to move in the direction of your dreams and desires.

Just like an overstuffed closet or an overflowing drawer, often a to-do list can be filled with too many tasks that become clutter. Be scrupulous with what you allow onto your to-do list, and know that, in addition to saying yes and doing a task with vigor, you have other options available, which are to eliminate, delay, or delegate. With that, there are three simple questions you can ask yourself.

- Does this need to be done today?
- Does this need to be done by me?
- Does this need to be done at all?

Learning to make decisions quickly will provide you with the fuel you need to move forward and get things done.

Delay: Does This Need to Be Done Today?

Do you sometimes get overwhelmed by your to-do list because it feels like everything on it needs to be done right now? It's not hard to believe you feel that way given our fast-paced, instant gratification culture.

Delaying a task or project isn't saying "no," it's saying "not now." If you find yourself overwhelmed by the number of items on your to-do list, then it's important to figure out whether they can be delayed.

It is important that you do not make assumptions regarding deadlines for projects or tasks. In my experience, often the requesters don't have clear deadlines in mind when they ask and use as soon as possible as a default. It's your responsibility to clarify deadlines before making a commitment and also to negotiate deadlines if you're finding your calendar and to-dos are not in alignment.

Here are a few questions to ask yourself when deciding if an item on your to-do list can be delayed:

- Do you really need to do it now? Write down the exact reason why you believe it does.
- What could go wrong if you don't do it now?
- Is there anyone else who believes this needs to be done now?
- Have you asked the person you believe cares that it is done now if it can be delayed?

Delegate: Does This Need to Be Done by Me?

Sometimes there are items on your to-do list that would be better for someone else to do. You can think about delegation in two ways.

The first is to delegate relatively simple tasks and projects to help you maximize your Q2 time. Look at some of your Q1 and Q3 tasks, and decide whether you could easily direct someone else to do those tasks to free yourself up.

CLIENT CHRONICAL: DROWNING IN TO-DOS

One person I coached, we'll call her Diana, was so overwhelmed with the size of her to-do list she could hardly talk about it without getting emotional. She believed everything she had on her to-do list was essential and needed to be done.

When we began to dig into each item one by one and I asked if it could be eliminated, she almost began to cry and said no. Item after item seemed impossible to take off the list completely, even though some, to me at least, seemed obvious contenders for elimination.

So, we started digging deeper and I asked Diana a series of simple questions. By peeling away some of the notion that everything had to be done no questions asked, she was able to successfully eliminate several of the to-dos from her list, which lifted a huge weight from her shoulders.

Once you know

what you need to do,

taking action at a time when

you will be

most productive

will create *wonderful* flow.

The second is to delegate items strategically to develop others and elevate their skills while, in turn, elevating the skills of the whole team—whether the team consists of family, coworkers, or friends. This type of delegation requires more planning and more support and can lead to a significant increase in Q2 time for you in the long run. Strategically delegating to grow others provides significant rewards in the end.

Delegation can be hard for many people because it requires trusting others as well as holding others accountable. Delegation also requires time, patience, and practice, which is difficult to feel you have time for when you're already overloaded. However, it is essential to learn to delegate effectively.

Eliminate: Does This Need to Be Done at All?

If you find items on your to-do list that are not worth the time invested, then take them off your list. We do not need to do everything we or someone else thinks of, period.

If you struggle to eliminate items from your to-do list, it might be likely that you're having a hard time determining what is truly important and what is not. Many people struggle with completely taking an item off the to-do list. You may feel as if taking it off means you've failed. Trust me, you haven't. You can feel proud when you're confident in what's important and then work only on those things.

Here are a few questions to ask yourself when deciding if an item on your to-do list can be eliminated:

- Do you *really* need to do it? Say why exactly.
- What would happen if you didn't do it? Who would care?
- Could anyone else do it? If not, why not?

By digging deeper into each to-do rather than blindly doing it, we put the power of choice back into our hands. I challenge you to look at your current to-do list and find one or two things you can eliminate completely. You will begin to see that even though you might have believed it was not possible to eliminate it without retribution, indeed it actually was.

Find a Planner That Works for You

If you've never used a planner consistently, it's time to really consider it. Trying to manage daily to-dos without a system is very difficult, and once you find a planner that works for you, you'll find that the stress of knowing what you need to do and when is cut down considerably.

Finding a planner that works for you can be like finding the right pair of jeans. It will take patience and trying on a few different options before you find what works best. If planners have not worked for you in the past, don't give up! It's also important for you to consider what hasn't worked for you in the past and why.

Rule number one when considering a planner is to look for one planner that meets all of your needs rather than having several. Trying to manage a notebook for notes, another for a journal, another for a calendar, and another for kids' activities requires your brain to have to remember and shift and adjust too much and isn't ideal. Simplification is key.

The planner you will choose will depend on what you're going to use the planner for. Are you a working parent who needs to keep track of various meetings and appointments throughout the day along with kids' activities? Are you a mom who needs to track kids' appointments and coordinate play and learning activities? Do you need to track birthdays and anniversaries? What about taking notes and/or planning ahead? Do you want to be able to journal in your planner? Do you need to track food or habits or activities? Do you have large or small handwriting that might dictate the size of the planner? Do you prefer to have an online calendar?

● *Picking one planner that works for you is essential to gaining a clearer focus of everything in one place.*

At the most basic level, a planner is simply a tool to help you keep track of three main things:

1. what you need to remember (important dates, appointments, notes)
2. what you need to do (tasks and appointments)
3. what you're thinking about (life goals, aspirations, ideas)

The goal of a planner is to help you make the best use of your time and energy. And remember, a planner doesn't have to be an elaborate binder with endless tabs. It can be a simple analog or digital notebook that records everything. The importance of whatever planner system you choose is that it is all in one spot and that it works for you.

Take Action (Try Using a Weekly Planner)

Once you've determined the tasks or projects you need to do, it's time to take action. It's time to put them on your to-do list, block off time on your calendar to focus on them, and get the tasks done. To do this, you will put the theories we've reviewed in this chapter into action.

Let's review an example of what to do when planning out one week.

First, grab your new planner and find a comfortable spot where you will be uninterrupted. Then, looking at the quadrant you created for all of the tasks and projects, write down the ones that you are able to complete in one week based on the time estimates you've made for each task.

Start by writing down your Q2 tasks onto weekly planner pages and writing your time estimates next to the tasks. You can use one pen or pencil to do this, but if you're a visual learner, consider using different colors for the different quadrants of tasks.

Once you have written down your Q2 tasks, write down your Q1 and Q3 tasks. It's important not to forget the tasks or projects you've chosen to delegate as you will need to make time to communicate and be available for questions.

CLIENT CHRONICAL:
TOO MANY NOTEBOOKS

One of my clients, we'll call her Jenny, was overwhelmed with everything she had to do. She hired me to help her go through many piles of papers that were on almost every flat surface in the house.

When we started sorting through all of the papers, I noticed she had a lot of notebooks and slips of papers with small notes on them. I shared that I thought maybe having so many notebooks was getting in the way of her staying on top of her to-dos. She listened to me but didn't really see my point. So I decided to show her what I saw.

I gathered up all of the notebooks into one spot—there were about thirty in various sizes and about a 2-inch (5 cm) stack of individual sheets of paper with notes on them. When I showed her the volume of notebooks and slips of papers, she couldn't believe her eyes. She hadn't realized how she would just grab a notebook, any notebook, to write down a to-do and then would lose track of it.

I recommended she go on the hunt to find one planner that worked for her and use it consistently. Doing this helped her simplify considerably, allowing her to be more focused and more effective in managing her to-dos.

week of

	monday	tuesday	wednesday

TO DO

MEAL PLAN

HABIT TRACKER

habit	m	t	w	th	f	s	su

Weekly Planner

thursday	friday	saturday

sunday

inspiration (quote/word/phrase)

notes:

Consistent Review and Reflection

Since there are so many things that can sidetrack you on the road to getting tasks done, it's important to be present as you go about your work. Ensure you are making time to review your progress throughout the day and throughout the week in order to keep yourself on track.

Even the best planners get it wrong from hour to hour and day to day. It's not important that you fervently stick to your schedule; it's important that you make progress and move forward. If one task took you longer than you estimated, take it as a learning moment and provide yourself a little more cushion next time. If you find you're easily distracted, break up your tasks into fifteen-minute time blocks and be focused when you're working through them.

There are many tips for staying on task and maximizing your time, but the most powerful one is to consistently review your to-do list to see how you are tracking and to see the progress you are making. This isn't something you need to do every half hour, but consistency is key to ensure you stay on track. It's especially important if you have a lot of mental clutter and find yourself unable to stay focused on one task at a time.

The importance of keeping your mind calm and focused (uncluttered), which we will dig into fully in the next chapter, is the single most important factor in the holistic guide to decluttering.

Decluttering Your Day Checklist

☐ **Write everything down.** Writing down what you need to get done is an important first step to ensure you have a full picture of what it is that you need to accomplish. It also transfers the burden of having to keep it all in your head.

☐ **Evaluate and prioritize.** Reviewing the list of things you wish to accomplish and determining each task's level of importance and level of urgency are critical parts of completing your to-do list.

☐ **Practice estimating time.** Estimating how much time it takes you to complete a task and then evaluating how accurate your time estimate was will make it easier for you to plan tasks in the future because you'll have a clearer picture of how long certain tasks take to complete.

☐ **Decide and do!** Decision and action are the two important ways to move items from your to-do list to your done list.

☐ **Find a planner that works for you.** Taking the time to look for and try out different planners to find the one that works for you can be a game changer in managing and taking back your time.

DECLUTTERING YOUR MIND

7

Decluttering unseen clutter is where true transformation lies.

There is nothing ordinary about your mind: It is one of the most wonderful, amazing, and extraordinary things there is. When harnessed, it has the power to do miraculous things.

By digging deep into your mental clutter, you can transform yourself to levels you might not be able to imagine. Cultivating your mind in a positive direction can literally change your life.

When your mind operates on autopilot (which, for many of us, is most of the time), you are selectively perceiving your experiences by interpreting them in a way that aligns with your existing beliefs, fears, hopes, and dreams. On autopilot, it's almost impossible for a different point of view to get through. Your expressions and behaviors are self-fulfilling prophesies of your mindset.

Having lived with a lot of mental clutter of my own, I now know the benefits of considering new approaches and getting off of autopilot. After working on decluttering mental clutter over the last decade, I'm excited to share some insights with you.

Neuroscientists use the term "neuroplasticity" to refer to the fact that our brains have the ability to change our synaptic wiring. This means we have the ability to intentionally change the way we think by forming new neural pathways through practice.

There are many ways to practice mindfulness to help decrease mental clutter, and in this chapter, you will dig into some of the options. To me, mindfulness is being present with my thoughts. It is being in the moment and mindful and aware of what I am doing. On the following pages, you will explore different types of mental clutter, how your brain works, and ways to declutter your mind through a variety of techniques. What's most exciting about mental decluttering is that it can be done anywhere and everywhere. You will look like the same person on the outside, but your mind will be transforming on the inside.

• *Mental clutter is the clutter that no one else can see.*

When we have

too much going on around us,

it's difficult for our minds

to settle and *focus*

on what we need to do.

How Mental Clutter Affects the Brain

I remember a family road trip we took from Minnesota to the Dakotas in the 1980s. In general, my family was noisy, but put the six of us in a car for an extended period of time and the noise hit a whole different level. There was one point during the trip where my parents got frustrated because we were lost; and when their frustration boiled over the edge, one of my parents yelled, "Be quiet! We can't even hear ourselves think!" They then commanded we stay silent until they knew we were on the right path.

It seemed odd to me that my parents needed silence just to look at a map, but it turns out their request was not as crazy as I once believed. As you go through your day, you collect information about your environment through your five primary senses. Each sensory system tells the central nervous system about changes they detect in the environment. This means your brain is constantly evaluating a hierarchy of tasks.

Your brain's ability to switch back and forth between tasks is called attention switching, but it's not instantaneous, which can slow down your reaction time. When you're lost, that could mean the difference between seeing or not seeing your exit.

This is why my parents couldn't think while they were trying to look at the map—between the radio playing and the noise of the kids, they were not able to concentrate on the primary task. Turning down the volume of what is coming at you helps you focus on the primary task.

Types of Mental Clutter

Decluttering your mind is not as easy as decluttering a linen closet. You're not able to take everything out, discard what you don't love, put like things together, and then put them back into the closet with beautiful labels. It certainly would be easier if that were possible! Let's look at a few examples of mental clutter that might derail or overwhelm you as well as a variety of ways you can begin to remove the clutter from your mind.

Note that I'm sharing a variety of solutions because not all of them will speak to you. I encourage you to try as many of the suggestions as seems right for you and to select at least one solution that makes you feel a little uncomfortable. Since our minds can often be on autopilot, taking a step into something uncomfortable (at least at first) might be just the thing you need to cut the clutter from your mind. With that, let's dig in.

Mental Clutter: Rushing Mind

Ever had a morning where it seemed as if the seconds on the clock were clicking along faster than normal? I think we've all had that feeling where for every one step we take forward, we feel like we're also taking two steps back.

You might be trying to focus on the task at hand like getting dressed and getting your hair brushed, but then a thought comes into your mind and distracts you. You begin thinking about something your kids need for school or that you need for work, so you rush to grab that item, leaving the bathroom without finishing what you started. Then you head back to finish getting dressed, and another thought comes into your mind about an important project at work, so you decide to quickly check your email. Several minutes later, you realize that way more time has passed than you thought and now you're going to be late. Since now your mind is thinking about being late, you begin rushing even more.

Let's investigate strategies to bring that overactive mind in check.

If you're constantly

on *overdrive,*

your mind can rush and

make your body feel

out of control.

CLIENT CHRONICAL: RUSHING THROUGH THE DAY

I observed one of my clients, we'll call her Renee, rushing from one place to the next as we worked. I also observed her rushing when she had to leave part of the session to pick up her son from school. After a couple of days of the fast talking and fast moving, I approached Renee with my observations.

When I shared my observations, she said it was absolutely true and she felt like she had been rushing her entire life. We dug in a little more, and I learned that often times her mind and her body were not working on the same task. She might be with me trying to sort through a certain category, but she would get distracted in her mind about something she felt she might be running late on and internally she began to rush.

I asked her to take a big inhale and a big exhale. We discussed the task she was working on and the different task she was thinking about. I shared with her that we had enough time to do both of those things, but we needed to do them one at a time. I set a timer for fifteen minutes and asked her to completely focus on the first task. Then, once that was finished, we set the timer for another fifteen minutes and focused on the second task.

She told me this simple change, addressing the rushing mind with a clear and easy plan, helped her mind and body relax; and she could focus on the first task she needed to get done and then the second.

Do One Thing at a Time

When you try to do many tasks without focusing your mind on one thing at a time, you decrease your ability to do them well. Multitasking also impedes the brain's ability to retain information.

The reality is that multitasking is not actually multitasking at all. Although you might think you're able to divide your focus among multiple tasks, your brain is actually just attention switching over and over.

So, one solution to help is to single task, which is the practice of dedicating yourself to one task at a time, minimizing potential interruptions until the task is complete or a select time period has elapsed.

While single tasking sounds easy, it's actually more difficult than you might suspect since your brain is working against you. You see, the region of the brain you need to rely on to stay on task—the prefrontal cortex—is the exact region of the brain that can be easily distracted.

Do Less

If you have booked every minute of your day for as far as the eye can see, there is a chance your mind is also fully booked and overflowing. This means you're probably a good candidate for doing less.

Doing less means simply that. Look at your calendar and pull some things off of it. You make the decision that some things can wait or never be done at all. Doing less doesn't mean you do nothing. It means that you may do fewer things, but more of what matters.

Think you can't do less? Think again. You are the driver of your time and your calendar and the curator of your life. Don't think you're ready for a full-scale do-less life? Try doing less for a month and see how it goes.

When you do less, you will have more energy and passion for the things you will do. You will also have less anxiety and stress around your every move. You can breathe a little deeper because you've given yourself a much-needed rest.

Breathe

There might be times when your mental clutter is so overwhelming that doing less is not enough. You need to make a more dramatic shift away from what you are doing and thinking, and simply stop. Literally, stop what you're doing and stop what you're thinking and just breathe.

Taking a few deep breaths can do a lot to help slow down your racing mind and help you focus. When you're stressed, your body can produce too much norepinephrine—a natural brain chemical messenger—making it difficult to focus.

Try it now. Close your eyes and slowly take ten deep breaths in through your nose and out through your mouth. Chances are you feel a little more focused and possibly calmer, but why?

Researchers at Trinity College Institute of Neuroscience and the Global Brain Health Institute found that focused breathing affects levels of norepinephrine and can enhance your attention to detail and improve your overall brain health.

Simply put, the researchers found that by focusing on and regulating your breathing, you can optimize your attention level; and likewise, by focusing your attention level, your breathing becomes more synchronized.

Turn Things Off

Only a few decades ago, a typical morning consisted of simply reading the morning paper with a cup of coffee. Sure, a few advertisements in the newspaper might distract you; but, for the most part, reading the newspaper was uninterrupted.

Today, you're more likely to read the news from your handheld mobile device while standing over a plate and waiting for the coffee to finish brewing. And, while you're scrolling through the news, there is good chance you'll see a mobile ad, hear the ping of an email or a text message, or possibly see an alert from your social media or an app.

You can minimize distractions by turning things off—notifications on your phone, email alerts, your radio, your TV. Take an inventory of how many things are turned on in the morning when you are getting ready for work or in the evening when you're trying to relax and go to bed. Turning a few things off might be just the respite your brain needs.

• *Deep breathing when you are anxious or overwhelmed can help reset your mind and remind your body that everything is okay.*

Mental Clutter: Negative Nelly

Have you ever found yourself dwelling on an insult you've received or fixating on a mistake you've made? Your mind gets in a negative loop, and you're not even sure how it started in the first place, but it made you unhappy.

It is very common to experience this Negative Nelly disposition, as I call it. Psychologists refer to it as a negativity bias, which is our tendency to register negative stimuli more readily and also to dwell on those events longer. When you consider the other research studies that suggest we need to hear between four and seven positive comments to balance a negative one, the negativity bias makes sense.

Because the "bad things" grab our attention and stick to our memories, in many cases, we dwell on them longer. They can take up a lot of space in our minds and become clutter.

Negative thoughts playing on a loop in our minds is another example of mental clutter. Let's explore ways to declutter our minds from Negative Nelly.

Find Your Compassionate Inner Voice

Everyone has an inner critic. For some, the critic is under control and easily managed. For others, the inner critic is a very loud voice and can lead to a lot of mental clutter. There are many different ways the inner critic can show up, from being the judge "I can't believe you cannot figure out how to do this!" to the nag "Seriously, can't you just get up and take care of this right now?" to the bully "Is that really what you're going to wear to this event?" The inner critic can be very harsh.

What we know from the practice of psychology is that it's likely the inner critic comes from early life experiences that are internalized and taken in as ways we think about ourselves.

Learning to turn off the internal critic will help remove a lot of mind clutter.

Bring awareness to your strong inner critic. When you notice him or her creep into your head, stop yourself, try to shift your thinking, and use a compassionate inner voice to see the situation in a new light.

One way to think about what a compassionate inner voice sounds like is to ask yourself: What would I say to a friend who was in this same situation? Often, the way we would talk to a close friend is very compassionate and caring rather than critical and scolding.

The great news is that, over time, you can change the voice in your head to be less critical. It requires you to be mindful and aware of how you are talking to yourself. When you find yourself using a condemning voice, simply adjust the voice in your mind to be more compassionate.

Be Quick to Forgive

Anger is a human emotion that is physiologically beneficial, and getting upset from time to time will not do you any mental or physical harm. But if the frequency, duration, or intensity of your anger is significant, it can take a toll on your mind as well as on your long-term health.

The reason anger has such an effect is because when your mind is filled with negative thoughts and emotions, those thoughts take up your mental bandwidth and can send you down a negative spiral. I'm sure we've all experienced the dangerous spiral that happens when someone does something that sets off your anger in the morning and then, for the rest of the day, everything seems to be tainted in its wake.

Here is the thing about anger and resentment toward others: You have two choices—you can live in anger and resentment, or you can embrace forgiveness and move forward. While forgiveness means different things to different people, generally it is making a decision to let go of resentment and thoughts of revenge. It is a decision to let what is in the past stay in the past.

Research supports the fact that forgiveness can have significant health benefits, such as reduced anxiety and depression. The practice of forgiving not only reverses the resentment but also significantly decreases the other negative psychological concomitants that accompany the toxicity of resentment.

Celebrate More

I grew up in a family where we celebrated birthdays and a few other milestone events, but we certainly didn't celebrate Tuesday or tacos or other small-scale events. I didn't think much of it until I met a woman at work who seemed to celebrate everything.

At first, I didn't understand this woman. She woo-hoo'd loudly in meetings for seemingly mundane things, she celebrated small milestones with her team with baked goods and fun trinkets, and her birthday month was one long celebration. What I learned was that her celebration habit started in her childhood. Her parents celebrated the little things, the big things, and everything in between.

The wonderful thing is that your background doesn't matter. You can make a choice to celebrate more, and there are many benefits for doing so.

When you celebrate, you tend to create more lasting memories because the mind recalls memories easier when they are tied to strong emotional elements like a celebration. Celebrating also adds fun and excitement to your life. Celebrating can help you increase your personal connections because you are more likely to invite others to the celebration, making it even more meaningful.

One of the biggest reasons to celebrate more is that you will begin to hone your gratitude awareness as you look for things that deserve a toast, which might be as mundane as making it to Friday without losing your keys. When you begin to look for positive events and celebrate more, you will find your life being filled with much more enthusiasm and joy.

Learn to recognize

when it's time

to give your mind a *break*.

Mental Clutter: Decision Fatigue

Making decisions, even small ones, can wear you down over time. Every day you need to make decisions from the moment you wake until the moment you go to sleep. And some days, the number of decisions you need to make is significantly greater than others, which leads to mind clutter. Every decision requires your time and energy and can deplete your willpower. This phenomenon is called decision fatigue, and it depletes your mental energy. Being low on mental energy can lead to mental clutter.

Set Limits

A very effective way to combat decision fatigue and the mind clutter that goes with it is to set limits for yourself throughout the day. Some examples of setting limits are as follows:

- **Set a time limit.** By setting a timer, you give yourself a very clear target for when you need to make the decision or for when you will need to finish something. This takes advantage of what we know as Parkinson's Law, which is that "work expands so as to fill the time available for its completion."

- **Set a choice limit.** Having too many choices can create mental clutter because of the number of options running through your mind at a given moment. You might become ultrafocused on the decision-making process and second-guess yourself due to the sheer number of options and alternatives. One way to combat this mind clutter is to limit your choices by saying you will only look at a certain number of options, and then make the choice from that limited set and move on.

Eliminate Choice

There are times when eliminating choice can really simplify your life and, in turn, your decision-making. Some examples of eliminating your choices might include the following:

- **Choose a work uniform.** Wear the same kind of outfit every day.

- **Eat the same thing every week.** Set a meal plan for each day and stick with it.

- **Eat the same thing every day.** A more extreme option, you could choose to eat the exact same thing every day to limit choice.

Delegate Decisions

If you find yourself with too many decisions, one thing you can do to ease the clutter in your mind is simply to delegate the decision. Don't want to decide what to eat at a restaurant? Then ask your waiter to make a suggestion. Don't want to decide the best dress to wear to a party? Then ask a friend to pick one out for you. Those are just a couple of examples of how you can delegate decisions.

The key to delegating decisions is to fully let the decision-making go and to take whatever decision your deligated person made.

Something as *simple* as

a cup of coffee

each morning

can be a nice morning ritual

to get your day started

on the right foot.

Daily Rituals and Routines

There are many tools to help you declutter your mind. So many tools, in fact, that it can be overwhelming to know where to get started. I'm going to share my top suggestions for clearing mental clutter.

Find a Mantra

A mantra is a sound, word, or phrase that helps you keep your mind focused. When you keep your mind focused on the mantra, it can help reduce the mind chatter. This technique is often used in yoga or a meditation practice, but it can have far-reaching uses.

Take a few deep breaths and repeat your mantra until your mind stops racing. Using a mantra helps redirect your thoughts and helps keep you present.

The options for mantras are limitless and can change whenever you feel they need to. They can be adapted to fit the need you have at the moment whether it be the need to focus, to motivate yourself, to calm yourself, or to simply be present. Some examples of mantras include:

- Be here right now.
- Breathe.
- I am enough.
- I give myself permission to slow down.
- I can, I will.

Keep a Journal

Journaling has many benefits, but an important one is that it helps you relax your mind. Writing in a journal can help you put what is going on in your head onto paper. By doing so, you can work through unresolved conflict by analyzing and organizing your thoughts. Simply stated, it can help you stop the thoughts from swirling around in your mind.

Writing in a journal can also improve working memory, according to research published in the *Journal of Experimental Psychology: General*. The study suggests that expressive writing eliminates intrusive thoughts about negative events, which improves working memory. The research also suggests that these improvements might free up our cognitive resources for other mental activities, including the ability to manage stress more effectively.

Meditate

On the simplest level, meditation is a technique used to rest your mind. When you meditate, you are fully awake and alert but your mind is not focused on events taking place around you or on a list of things you need to do. Meditation requires your mind to be still and be silent.

There are many different ways to try meditation, from following a guided meditation video or a meditation app to going to a meditation class or reading about it and just trying it out for yourself.

Meditation causes your brain and nervous system to undergo radical changes that reduce anxiety and depression as well as increase stress resilience. What's amazing is that over time you can train yourself to meditate anywhere, even if it is just for a few seconds. Simply telling yourself to focus on your breath for a few moments might be enough to remove some of the clutter filling your mind.

The guided meditation worksheet at right will help you get started.

Guided Meditation Worksheet

Set a gentle-sounding timer on your phone for two minutes, and then close your eyes.

Take a slow, deep inhale through your nose, and then a complete exhale through your mouth.

Continue breathing in a slow and steady manner with your eyes closed.

Bring awareness of your breath. Start to notice what thoughts are going through your mind.

What are you thinking about?

Do not get caught up in your thoughts, but just begin to notice them as they travel across your mind. Let them go as they pass, and watch them come and go.

As you continue to breathe deeply, slowly count your inhales and exhales until you get to ten. You can also silently say "breathe in" in your mind as you inhale and "breathe out" as you exhale if this is better for you than counting.

If your mind wanders off, don't judge your thoughts. Just watch them float by in your mind and continue counting breathing in and breathing out.

Continue to breathe in and out until you hear the timer on your phone.

Take a last slow, deep inhale and a long, complete exhale.

Open your eyes.

EXPAND YOUR TRIBE

It's a reality in life that some people hold you back, while others help move you forward. If you spend most of your time with closed-minded and negative people, it's difficult to maintain a positive and open mindset.

Consider for a moment the five people with whom you spend most of your time. Would you consider those people positive influences? Are they your champions? Are they people you admire? Do they support you?

The people you choose to spend the most time with will shape who you are. They will affect your attitude and, in turn, your behaviors. It's human nature.

It is also why it might be time for you to evaluate your current tribe and consider expanding it in order to line up with where you are headed.

As you head into the holistic decluttering journey, you will want to surround yourself with champions. Doing so will help keep you accountable as well as help motivate you when you need an extra boost and will give you someone to celebrate with.

Finding a tribe

that loves and supports you

while you love and support them

can be life-altering and

joyful.

IT'S OKAY TO GET HELP

If you feel your mental clutter is really limiting your ability to move forward, it might be time to add another member to your tribe: Seek out professional help from a therapist, doctor, or both. Anxiety, depression, and ADHD all add to mind clutter.

If you suspect you have or have been diagnosed with ADHD or another disorder, seeking professional help will help connect you with professionals who are trained to help you thrive. I've had many clients who have been diagnosed with ADHD. They work with me to help them declutter their spaces, and they work with an additional professional to help them come up with strategies to manage mind clutter.

Even if you don't have ADHD, seeking therapy may be worthwhile. Personally, I have experienced that the help of mental health professionals is remarkable. If you've never tried it, now might be a good time. If you've tried it and didn't seem to find the right person to help, it might have been a bad fit. You can try again.

Decluttering Your Mind Checklist

- [ ] **Slow down and do less when you need to.** Being present and aware of when you need to slow down and do less when it's appropriate will be imperative as you begin to be more intentional with your life.

- [ ] **Use breath work to slow your mind.** When you have an overactive mind, use breathwork to help calm your mind and body so that you can see things with a clearer perspective.

- [ ] **Find your compassionate inner voice.** Talking to yourself the way you would talk to a good friend is what is needed to help you make changes in a positive direction.

- [ ] **Set parameters around decisions to avoid fatigue.** When your mind gets tired, it becomes more difficult to make decisions. It's important for you to put some parameters in place that help you be productive when you need to be and rest when it's necessary.

- [ ] **Use rituals and routines to help you stay focused.** Rituals and routines are wonderful ways to help use your mind and muscle memory to stay focused and get things done quickly.

THE JOURNEY CONTINUES

Stepping stones of hope are what you need to carry you forward.

I'm excited for everyone who makes the commitment to a holistic decluttering journey. As you clear the clutter from your space, your time, and your mind, you will feel different—in a good way. If you have already started, you've no doubt noticed how you are already seeing things from a different persepective. Along the way, you have learned new things about yourself, remembered things you might have forgotten, and, hopefully, shed some bad habits as well.

But like many of life's journeys, the holistic decluttering path is never straight. It includes unexpected turns and twists. And it is more about the path itself than the destination. For example, you might have found it very easy to declutter one category in your home, while you've struggled with another. You might have moved a few steps forward when it comes to time clutter but then reverted to some old habits. All of this is normal. You should see it as a call for a little more practice, and make some adjustments.

Whatever you do, don't give up.

In this chapter, you will find guidance for things I have found helpful for myself and for my clients when it comes time to maintain your hard-fought victories. Some of these suggestions are practical and focus more on the home, while others may help you maintain peace in other areas of your life. There is no need to follow all the advice—try something out and see what works for you and your family.

• *For all things in life, let's measure our progress rather than in perfection.*

Embrace Simplicity

When you remove clutter from your life, it requires maintenance on your part to keep new clutter from piling up. The best tool you have to keep clutter from returning to your home, your calendar, and your mind is to be present and aware. If you've had difficulties staying present in the past, you will find it becomes a little easier when you decrease the noise around you by decluttering. Your life without as much clutter will feel simpler.

My advice is to embrace this newfound simplicity with gusto. Embracing simplicity doesn't mean you will lose out on what matters most. It means you will continue to be aware of, and not allow into your life, what matters least. It means listening and reacting to your internal guide when your space, calendar, or mind begins to feel clutter creep back in. It's about knowing yourself well enough to know your limits.

This doesn't mean you don't take on new things or try something that might shake up your newfound balance. It's about embracing a buy-what-you-can-manage and do-what-you-can-manage lifestyle. This will be different for everyone. Some of you will feel very comfortable managing a lot at once, while others will feel overwhelmed more quickly. Some of you might be in a season where it's easy to take on more, while others might feel quite the opposite and feel the need to pull back. It's about you, your life, and what is going on at the moment. However, no matter your personality or bandwidth, there are a few key areas where less is definitely more.

Simplifying home décor, like placing just a few fresh-cut flowers in glass jars, is a way to showcase something you love without introducing visual clutter.

> If you're barely able to *Manage* what you have, it's time to consider buying less.

Buy Less

Buying less has many benefits: You'll save money and time and will reduce your carbon footprint. When it comes to clutter management, the biggest benefit of buying less is that you will have fewer things to manage. If you're unable (or barely able) to manage what you currently have, it's time to consider buying less.

Buying less may not always save you money. It might mean that you are buying higher-quality items, but fewer of them. Many people find they become more intentional about their buying after they have decluttered. By being more selective about what you choose to buy, you'll become a true curator, surrounding yourself only with things you love—and things that will last. You might also consider adopting "no buy" periods on nonessentials. I have known people who have tried this for a week, a month, or even a year.

If you find you are saving money, you could soon be using the money you've saved for other things, like traveling or other experience-related activities. A lot of people who begin to buy less are amazed by how much more of life they can experience with this one simple change.

"Should" Yourself Less

I imagine you've shoulded yourself into doing many things you don't really want to do. For example, you might say things like "I should go to so-and-so's party" or "I should exercise more" or even "I should spend more time with my family."

If you observe yourself for a couple of days, you'll probably see that you should yourself more than you realized. You might also observe that you should yourself in areas you believe you're lacking in some way. (Often, should is used as a motivator to move a person into action, learned during adolescence.)

The challenge when you compel yourself into action so frequently is that you lose your ability to distinguish the difference between what you want to do and what you should do. Living days and weeks filled mostly with shoulds can lead to resentment and low self-esteem.

When you fill your days with more things that you want to do rather than those you simply believe you should do, it feels different. Sometimes, that difference is a matter of perspective. If you have a goal to improve your health, you could say "I should go to the gym since I haven't gone in a while." With a different perspective, you might say instead "I want to feel better, so I'm going to do some activity today that will get my heart pumping" and see where the road leads you. Maybe you'll end up at the gym, but maybe you'll end up having a dance party or going on a hike.

Of course, as a responsible adult, there are things you need to do and might not really want to do, like paying bills. I'm not suggesting you throw responsibility out the window here. I'm simply suggesting you become more aware of when and why you are using this mindset in order to get in touch with yourself and find what truly motivates you into action.

One way to move away from the should lifestyle is to give yourself time each day for should-free zones. Spend time considering only what your heart wants, and chase that for some time. You might discover, to your own surprise, there are some things you never imagined wanting to do and some things that motivate you better than any "should" ever would!

Rush Less

In this fast-paced world, it often seems people need to move fast in order to get things done. For some, rushing is actually connected to poor time management. For others, rushing is connected to excessive time urgency, often called "hurry sickness," which means you are tied to the clock and trying to do too many things at once.

No matter the cause, all of this rushing can lead to a greater risk of cardiovascular and other health-related problems because the body is constantly at a high anxiety and stress level. The good news is there are many stratagies to try to rush less. Here are a few:

- **Slow down.** If you find the pace of your steps and heartbeats moving faster from rushing around, purposefully slow down your steps as well as your breathing. Walking slower and breathing slower will slow down your brain as well.

- **Be realistic.** While it is important to be on time for most appointments, not all of them require a do-or-die attitude. Rushing though traffic and yelling at everyone along the way to get to an appointment for which you could have been a few minutes late with no real consequences is a choice. Controlling your expectations can go a long way in rushing less.

- **Leave a margin.** Giving youself a little bit more room in your time estimates will give you the space you need to do what you need to do (and when you need to do it by). This includes estimating how much time it will take you to move from one task, or one appointment, to another. Remember the adage: "The hurrier I go, the behinder I get."

Worry Less

For some people, their grip is simply too tight. They are overcommitted, overcontrolling, and have too much on their plates. And if that weren't enough, they worry about everyone and everything, which leaves them in a constant state of stress and anxiety.

If this sounds like you, it's time for you to loosen your grip. In other words, it's time to consider how you can let go of some things and go with the flow more. If you're not a natural go-with-the-flow person, this can be hard (trust me, I know from personal experience). I hope you will learn what I've learned by worrying less and going with the flow more: The path can often take you to places that are better than you first considered or planned.

One way to loosen your grip is to simply cast your worries to the universe or to the God you embrace. By giving something up that bothers you while still holding steady in the faith in the future, you may find you have more peace in your heart and mind. And, in turn, you will have more space to do the things you really want to do.

A slow, deep breath
is a *powerful*
antidote to rushing.

Embrace Routine

Love them or hate them, routines are powerful tools that can help you thrive—especially after you remove the physical, time, and mental clutter. Counter to some popular beliefs, embracing routines does not need to be the end of spontaneity. Routines can actually open up space in your life for more spontaneity.

You might hear the words "routine" and "habit" interchangeably, but they actually mean different things. Understanding the definitions can help you design powerful routines as well as build strong habits. The primary difference between a routine and a habit is your level of personal consciousness. A routine is a series of behaviors, created by you, that requires you to practice it for it to become regular. A habit, on the other hand, usually shows up as an automatic urge to do something and is often triggered by a particular cue. Habits are how the brain learns to do things without forethought.

Both routines and habits are regular and repeated, but routines require a higher degree of intention and effort, whereas habits happen with little or no conscious thought. You can, with practice and commitment, turn a routine into a habit so the routine becomes automatic.

Of course, you can create routines for a multitude of different habits you're trying to create; but, in the spirit of simplicity, I recommend you start by focusing on the most powerful routines that can help you during the holistic decluttering journey. Perhaps they will help you move forward and continue to live an uncluttered life!

Morning Routine

Your morning routine is probably the most important routine you can establish. Having a thoughtful morning routine can help you create the momentum to have consistently great days. There are as many variations on morning routines as there are people, yet there are some consistencies in what makes a strong morning routine.

I'm a convert to laying my clothes out the night before. Anything to make my morning easier!

A FRESH APPROACH TO
THE MORNING

One of my clients found herself not being able to get to some priorities she'd set for herself such as meditation, prayer, and exercise. She felt defeated at the end of the day because she couldn't get them done.

Since she was a morning person, I suggested that she consider adding these priorities to her morning routine. This way, she could get them done in the morning when she was fresh, and then go on with her day not feeling as if things were hanging over her. I also encouraged her to get an accountability buddy who could check in every morning to see how she was doing with building her morning routine into a habit.

After many weeks of working with her accountability partner, she sounded completely different to me when we spoke. She was proud of how, with dedicated time in the morning and an accountability partner, she was able to stick to her goals and felt amazing because of it.

Consistent wake up time. When you wake up at the same time every day, you stabilize your circadian rhythm, which is basically your 24-hour internal clock. As a result, you will likely find you naturally become tired at the same time each night. Finding your best wake-up time will be based on what works best for your body and your schedule.

Eat breakfast. Breakfast is an important meal because it breaks your overnight fast period, replenishes your glucose, and kick-starts your metabolism.

Create an order for getting ready. The things you do to get ready each day, like getting dressed, brushing your teeth, and so on, can be done with more muscle memory and more quickly if you do them in a consistent order.

Prioritize the day's focus. It's best to skip checking your emails and texts until you've completed your morning routine as they can derail your focus—and sometimes your day. Taking time as part of your morning routine to prioritize what you will focus on during the day will help keep your mind clear of mental clutter and focused on your most important tasks.

Evening Routine

Much like the morning routine, having an evening routine can prove valuable. It can even help you get a good night's rest. Here are some ideas that may help you build a strong evening routine.

Create a winding down ritual. Creating a getting-ready-for-bed ritual helps tell your brain and body what's coming next. It might include washing your face, brushing your teeth, and getting your pajamas on. Start this ritual at least an hour before bed to give your body the time and space it needs to wind down.

Be mindful of food and drink. Pay attention to what you eat and drink in the evening. Going to bed on an empty stomach might keep you up later, and too much food or drink might create the need for a midnight trip to the bathroom. Avoid stimulants like nicotine and caffeine for four to six hours before bedtime as it takes hours to wear off (making it harder to fall—and stay—asleep).

Create a restful bedroom. Having a bedroom that is quiet, cool, and dark is more conducive to sleep. Removing clutter and potential stress triggers from the bedroom is also important. One way to keep the bedroom restful is to give yourself a few minutes during your morning routine to make your bed and to tidy up a bit so that when you come back at night to rest, it's relaxing rather than messy.

Ditch the electronics. Using electronic devices before bed delays your body's circadian rhythm and suppresses the release of the sleep-inducing hormone melatonin, making it more difficult to fall asleep. Additionally, electronics might ping and beep while you sleep, reminding you of nagging to-dos. Best to ditch the electronics while in bed so your body can do what it needs to do and rest.

Relax. Consider ways to relax your body and mind once you're in bed and ready to rest. You might consider reading, writing in your journal, or writing down thoughts in your calendar for things you need to do the next day. Trying and finding what is best to help you relax will help you get a good night's sleep.

Prize Progress over Perfection

As a recoving perfectionist, it took me some time to learn the importance of progress over perfection. (Truth be told, I'm still working on it.) Perfection suggests a state of flawlessness, without any defects. You might be able to achieve perfection on a single task, like getting a perfect score on a test, but aiming for perfection in your life simply isn't achievabale. As humans, we were not designed to be perfect.

Progress, on the other hand, is something everyone can achieve. It is as simple as making movement or improvement from one day to the next in the direction of your goals and dreams. Keep in mind that progress can show up in a variety of ways, including a failure or a setback. When you are seeking progress over perfection, a failure or a setback provides useful lessons and feedback—even if it's painful.

So, as you embrace this decluttering journey, use progress as your yardstick. Before you know it, you'll be looking back at a remarkable journey of personal transformation and change.

Nurturing children from a young age to put their things away is an important life skill. So, it's important to embrace the way they would like to do it, knowing that it might not be perfect but that they are making progress.

The Journey Continues Checklist

☐ **Be present in the journey.** It's easy to look ahead and behind, but then we miss the moment we are living in now. Being present in the journey will make the finish line even sweeter.

☐ **Embrace simplicity.** When life is too complicated, it can shut you down. Embrace simplicity wherever you can so you have the ability to enjoy more of what's around you.

☐ **Embrace doing less of certain behaviors.** When you buy less, should yourself less, rush less, and worry less, you will feel the release of burdens from your calendar and from your mind. Doing so will open you up to live your most desired life.

☐ **Create morning and evening routines.** Establishing morning and evening routines can really set you up for some productive and fulfilling days ahead.

☐ **Prize progress over perfection.** Celebrating the progress you make along the way is far more important than trying to get everything perfect.

● *Stop to enjoy the views along your journey and appreciate small victories.*

Resources

Simplify Your Life: 100 Ways to Slow Down and Enjoy the Things That Really Matter,
Elaine St. James

One of the first books I read on decluttering and simplifying, and it still has a spot on my bookshelf. It's a simple read with big impact.

Essentialism: The Disciplined Pursuit of Less, Greg McKeown

I love how McKeown clearly illustrates a way of thinking he calls The Way of The Essentialist. At its root, The Essentialist is someone who learns how to do less, but do it better, and is able to weed out the noise.

The Life-Changing Magic of Tidying Up: The Japanese Art of Decluttering and Organizing, Marie Kondo

Kondo showcases a new approach to decluttering by putting joy at the center of your decision, which I found to be a simple, but effective, way of determining what items you choose to keep in your life.

Headspace app, Andy Puddicombe

Headspace is a wonderful meditation app for beginners. It was a treat to listen to Andy's calm voice in my early days of meditation and to follow his guidance for decluttering and bringing clarity to my mind.

Calm App, Michael Acton Smith and Alex Tew

Calm is a far-reaching mindfulness app that incudes meditation, daily mood check-ins, and sleep stories to help you wind down at night.

The Container Store

An amazing resource for when you have finished decluttering and you need bins and boxes to organize your new space.

References

Chapter 1

Keeping as a Source of Clutter | Attachment
Bruce M. Hood, Paul Bloom. "Children prefer certain individuals over perfect duplicates," *Cognition*, Volume 106, Issue 1 (2008): 455–462. https://doi.org/10.1016/j.cognition.2007.01.012

Chapter 2

The Grip of Physical Clutter | Women and Depressed Mood
Saxbe, Darby E., and Rena Repetti. "No Place Like Home: Home Tours Correlate With Daily Patterns of Mood and Cortisol." *Personality and Social Psychology Bulletin* 36, no. 1 (2009): 71–81. https://doi.org/10.1177/0146167209352864.

The Grip of Physical Clutter | Clutter Triggering Unhealthy Choices
Scheier, Michael F., Jagdish K. Weintraub, and Charles S. Carver. "Coping with Stress: Divergent Strategies of Optimists and Pessimists." *Journal of Personality and Social Psychology* 51, no. 6 (1986): 1257–64. https://doi.org/10.1037/0022-3514.51.6.1257.

Gain Clearer Focus | Decluttered Workspaces
McMains, Stephanie, and Sabine Kastner. "Interactions of Top-Down and Bottom-Up Mechanisms in Human Visual Cortex," *The Journal of Neuroscience* 31, no. 2 (2011): 587–97. doi:10.1523/ JNEUROSCI.3766-10.2011

Help Your Children Focus Too | Children's Classrooms
Fisher, Anna V., Karrie E. Godwin, and Howard Seltman. "Visual Environment, Attention Allocation, and Learning in Young Children." *Psychological Science* 25, no. 7 (2014): 1362–70. https://doi.org/10.1177/0956797614533801.

Save Time | "Lost & Found" Survey
Pixie Technology Inc. "Lost and Found: The Average American Spends 2.5 Days Each Year Looking For Lost Items Collectively Costing U.S. Households $2.7 Billion Annually in Replacement Costs." PR Newswire, June 26, 2018. https://www.prnewswire.com/news-releases/lost-and-found-the-average-american-spends-25-days-each-year-looking-for-lost-items-collectively-costing-us-households-27-billion-annually-in-replacement-costs-300449305.html.

Save Money | Home Size
2015 Characteristics of New Housing, 2015 Characteristics of New Housing (2015). https://www.census.gov/construction/chars/pdf/c25ann2015.pdf.

How to Envision Your Desired Life | Write Down Goals
Gardner, Sarah, and Dave Albee. "Study Focuses on Strategies for Achieving Goals, Resolutions," Dominican University of California. https://www.dominican.edu/dominicannews/study-highlights-strategies-for-achieving-goals

Chapter 4

Divide the Kitchen into Zones | The "Kitchen Triangle"
Blakeley, Janice. "This Is STILL the Best Way to Design a Kitchen." *Architectural Digest*, 6 Nov. 2018, www.architecturaldigest.com/story/kitchen-triangle-best-way-to-design-a-kitchen.

Chapter 6

Decluttering Your Day | Working Less
Gershuny, J., and O. Sullivan. United Kingdom Time Use Survey, 2014–2015. Centre for Time Use Research, University of Oxford. UK Data Service. http://doi.org/10.5255/UKDA-SN-8128-1

Evaluate | Mere Urgency Study
Zhu, Meng, Rajesh Bagchi, and Stefan J Hock. "The Mere Deadline Effect: Why More Time Might Sabotage Goal Pursuit." *Journal of Consumer Research* 45, no. 5 (May 2018): 1068–84. https://doi.org/10.1093/jcr/ucy030.

Estimate | The Planning Fallacy
Buehler, Roger, Dale Griffin, and Johanna Peetz. "The Planning Fallacy." Advances in Experimental Social Psychology, 2010, 1–62. https://doi.org/10.1016/s0065-2601(10)43001-4.

Kahneman, Daniel. *Thinking, Fast and Slow*. New York: Farrar, Straus and Giroux, 2015.

Chapter 7

Breathe | Focused Breathing
Melnychuk, Michael Christopher, Paul M. Dockree, Redmond G. Oconnell, Peter R. Murphy, Joshua H. Balsters, and Ian H. Robertson. "Coupling of Respiration and Attention via the Locus Coeruleus: Effects of Meditation and Pranayama." *Psychophysiology* 55, no. 9 (2018). https://doi.org/10.1111/psyp.13091.

Keep a Journal | Working Memory
Klein, Kitty, and Adriel Boals. "Expressive Writing Can Increase Working Memory Capacity." *Journal of Experimental Psychology: General* 130, no. 3 (2001): 520–33. https://doi.org/10.1037/0096-3445.130.3.520.

Acknowledgments

I have to start by thanking my wonderfully patient and loving husband, Dan. Without him, this book would not exist. Thank you for your constant support, your constant belief in me, and your steady nature to balance out my crazy. I'm deeply grateful for you. I'm especially thankful for you providing me with constant care after my knee surgery, allowing me to focus on healing and finishing the manuscript. I love you beyond words.

Thanks to my unique-as-snowflakes kids Julia and Owen. You both provide me with constant opportunities to see the world through a new (and often better) lens, providing me with a greater perspective on life, and pushing me to go outside my comfort zone and have a little more fun. I'm grateful and I love you both.

I've been blessed with a group of friends who provide both moral support and tough love when I need it, and I'm grateful for both parts as they've helped me grow. Special mention to Stephanie for knowing me before I knew myself and sticking with me since the 80s. To Caryn, for living daily life with me even though we're thousands of miles apart. And to Alison, for helping me see that I am enough just as I am.

Thank you to everyone on the Quarto team who helped me learn and grow during this book-writing journey. Special thanks to my editor, Thom O'Hearn, as well as Meredith Quinn, Ellen Goldstein, and Anne Re.

A sincere thank you to Jes Lahay for sharing your amazing talent with me. Creating with you is always fun, but having you as the photographer for this book was a dream come true.

Thank you, Dad, for teaching me that a little more defense always helps on the basketball court and that being a girl doesn't need to stop me. Thank you, Mom, for the countless personal sacrifices you made to provide your four crazy kids with lives filled with opportunities. Thank you, Dave, Jeff, and Bryan, for treating me like one of the guys with years of love shown as torment—it helped me become the strong woman I am today.

About the Author

Michele Vig, an accomplished corporate executive for two decades, founded Neat Little Nest to follow her passion. She enjoys helping her clients declutter, organize, and build the lives they envision. Michele is certified in the KonMari decluttering method and is a member of the National Association of Productivity and Organizing Professionals. Along with her business, Michele been widely featured in the media and has been recognized as one of Minnesota's top 50 women in business. Michele lives in Edina, Minnesota, with her husband and family.

Index